WHAT

·····································

MONA LISA

·····································

KNEW

ALSO BY

DR. BARBARA MACKOFF

LEAVING THE OFFICE BEHIND

WHAT
....
MONA LISA
....
KNEW

A WOMAN'S GUIDE TO GETTING AHEAD IN BUSINESS BY LIGHTENING UP
....

THE BOLD, NEW STRATEGY FOR LESS STRESS AND MORE SUCCESS ON THE JOB

DR. BARBARA MACKOFF

LOWELL HOUSE
Los Angeles

CONTEMPORARY BOOKS
Chicago

Library of Congress Cataloging-in-Publication Data

Mackoff, Barbara.
What Mona Lisa knew : a woman's guide to getting
ahead in business by lightening up / Barbara Mackoff.
p. cm.
ISBN 0-929923-20-0
1. Success in business.   2. Humor.   3. Women in business.
I. Title.

HF 5386.M226   1990   90-6241
650.1 ' 082–dc20   CIP

Requests for such permissions should be addressed to:

LOWELL HOUSE
1875 CENTURY PARK EAST, SUITE 220
LOS ANGELES, CA 90067

PUBLISHER: JACK ARTENSTEIN
VICE-PRESIDENT/EDITOR-IN-CHIEF: JANICE GALLAGHER
MARKETING MANAGER: ELIZABETH WOOD
DESIGN: HEIDI FRIEDER

Manufactured in the United States of America
10 9 8 7 6 5 4 3 2 1

For my father, Sam Mackoff
For my daughter, Hannah Miranda
And always, for Jeremy

WITHDRAWN

CONTENTS

ACKNOWLEDGMENTS

....

As I wrote, my appreciation for the good humor of my family has grown. I have lovingly recognized the influence of my father, whose warm chuckle is one of my most cherished memories; my mother, for her gift of celebration; and my sisters, Valerie, Cora, and Mavis, who–in the course of a phone call–can turn me into a carefree, cackling teenager.

My special thanks to: Jane, who gracefully walks the line between loving friend and candid critic; Dr. Bob Lieppman and the nurses at 4-West, whose good humor helped me meet my deadline; my agent, Amy Berkower, for her commitment to finding the right home for this book; my editor, Janice Gallagher, for her marvelous intuition, vision, and enthusiasm; and my "translator," Darlene Cox, for her caring and careful preparation of the manuscript.

I am grateful to have met the hundreds of women whose laughter and lightness dance across these pages.

And thank you, Jeremy, for your absolute belief in this project and for showing me how humor can confront and comfort. Your ability to make me laugh continues to astonish me.

PART ONE

··

THE SECRETS OF
THE GOOD-HUMOR WOMAN

*C*HAPTER *O*NE

....

WHAT MONA
LISA KNEW

*I*was just 16 when actress Merle Oberon revealed the secret of her flawless skin. "I never smile," she confessed. "Smiling would give me wrinkles." For weeks, I imagined her as Catherine in *Wuthering Heights* and practiced saying, "Heathcliff, bring me some heather," as I tried to turn up the corners of my mouth without creating feathery laugh lines around my eyes.

In my 20s, women stopped smiling for other reasons: We were too angry. We couldn't sit through a movie or a staff meeting, listen to the news or a popular song, without snarling about sexism. Everything we saw reminded us of women's exploitation, our lack of power and opportunity. We entered the workplace in vast numbers, determined to be taken seriously, and we accepted the advice of management gurus: Smiling was a sign of appeasement—or seduction.

So we lashed out at men, at work and at home; we tested and blamed them. When they whistled, we hissed. "That's *not* funny," we said. "Tell me a story about a man and a woman that has a happy ending" was the bitter gauntlet in those days.

A FUNNY THING HAPPENED TO ME

By my mid-30s, I became convinced that women could no longer ignore the laughter in our lives. And then a funny thing happened to me during the flu season of 1984, on the spring morning when I presented the least successful management seminar of my career. This particular seminar was a demonstration for a government agency—one that could net me a lucrative contract for dozens more. I had intended to do some serious business, but instead I had my first glimpse of the ideas I can now share with you.

I had fortified myself against my flu symptoms with a fistful of over-the-counter drugs and I opened the session by querying the participants about their expectations for the seminar. As we circled the room, comments were tentative and friendly until I turned to a fiftyish man—his menacing tattoo revealed by a short-sleeved white shirt. "My expectation," he growled, "is that I don't want to be here." The group gasped and concentrated its gaze on me. I surprised myself and him by saying, "Well, since you *are* here, it looks like your worst expectation has been met." His surly expression vanished, he laughed loudly and listened intently for the rest of the morning.

Following the introductions, I planned to show a witty, provocative videotape to launch the day's discussion of listening skills. I turned out the lights, pressed the play button, and waited confidently for the tape to begin—and waited, and waited, and waited—until I realized that I had mistakenly erased the entire videotape. Bravely, I announced to the darkened room, "Well, that's the last time I loan my recorder to Rosemary Woods!" Everyone laughed, but it was clear that my seminar had "fiasco" written all over it.

I wish I could tell you that I got the contract; but instead, the payoff was in the lesson of lightness. As I replayed the seminar in my mind, I was struck with the power of humor to communicate—how my lightness had established my credibility with the surly student and allowed me to remain composed during the morning's mishaps. That evening, when I recounted my day to my husband, Jeremy, I began to joke about the mechanical failure, insisting that I could not so much as turn on the stereo, stove, or television. Ah, the power of comic relief in soothing the stress of my disappointment.

ALL IN THE FAMILY

This encounter with the power of mirth echoed the memorable sense of humor in my family circle: a mother who laughed with delicious abandon, a father who was an inventive storyteller—from "The Tales of Brownie Bear" when we were small, to his earthier stories of later years. I can still hear my three sisters and me, shrieking with laughter, after the fourth glass of wine one Passover evening 25 years ago. My younger sisters' voices had reached a familiar pitch—one where they sounded like two frenzied, cackling hens. My father then tried to reestablish decorum with a predictable line reserved for such occasions: "A loud laugh betrays an empty mind." After his mock-serious pronouncement, we all laughed even louder.

Ours was a family of inside jokes, of silly shorthand. When we were teenagers, three subjects preoccupied my parents: sex ("A beautiful act *only* when you are married"), drugs ("They lead to sex"), and cleaner rooms ("Why do we live in such a lovely house if you are going to be so messy?"). So often did these parental concerns take the form of lectures (sometimes even accompanied by articles from medical journals) that when Mom or Dad raised one of the three subjects, we would simply ask: "Lecture Number 3?"

When I went away to college, each of my phone calls home to Phoenix would close with a loving parental caution, "Keep your wits about you." From my father I learned to tell a joke; from my mother, how to recognize one. Yet in spite of the good humor in our family, my ability to "lighten up," to use humor as a perspective and a means of feeling at ease, required some on-the-job training.

I have to laugh when I recall that the early years of my career were spent as a "serious" woman—with my naturally curly hair straightened with a blow-dryer, and my words chosen as carefully as my "power" pumps. But one lucky day, a friend saw me giving a presentation to a group of blue-ribbon executives and commented about how "tired" I seemed. I realized in that instant that I wasn't tired, I was simply being overly serious, holding back my natural sense of humor and exuberant style. Shortly after, I symbolically banished the blow-dryer and made a point of expressing and enjoying myself when I worked with clients.

But how could I bring what I had learned into my teaching?

WOMEN WHO FROWN TOO MUCH

One evening, as I looked across the podium in my career development seminar for women, I saw a garden variety of working women: first-time supervisors, fast-track MBA students, 20-year-olds beginning a first job, and divorced women reentering the job market after 20 years. All of these women had one thing in common: They were haunted by the prospect of not being taken seriously. They marched into my seminar in monotone suits, frowning with grim determination. "When a woman smiles," they cautioned one another, "nobody listens."

As I heard them tell their tales of work, it seemed that many of these bright and talented women had confused being serious with being solemn. "Business is business," they said. "Laughter is a luxury we can't afford." They spoke of arriving early and working late, of brooding over their mistakes, of crying when criticized, or feeling paralyzed by taking risks. In an attempt to be "professional," they opted to conceal not only their sense of humor but also their family life and personal style.

I was heartened by the solid connections between women in their offices, but I was troubled by the genuine discomfort these women felt in working closely with men. They sought acceptance from men by demonstrating how "seriously" they took their jobs—concentrating on perfecting their work rather than building working alliances. They were angered or hurt by men's aggressive or "childish" humor, yet they worried about being excluded from it. Clearly these ambitious women were neglecting their sense of humor as a vital key for success and survival on the job. And a growing body of research pointed to the strong potential of "the good-humor woman."

I considered these facts: In a series of studies, 84 percent of personnel directors stated that employees with a sense of humor did a better job, and 98 percent of CEOs stated a preference for job candidates with a sense of humor. Yet, when 200 executives were asked to name the qualities that kept women from succeeding, *lack of a sense of humor was near the top of the list.*

By then, I was convinced that humor was serious business, especially for women on the job. I began to design a new seminar based on developing humor both as an attitude and as a professional tool. And for the past five years, in addition to "humoring" executives and staff of *Fortune* 500 companies like Kodak, IBM, and Du Pont, I've had the pleasure of guiding more than 4,000 working women in a course on the art of "lightening up."

In the chapters that follow, you'll discover the spirit and strategies of the good-humor woman, as well as the fears and limitations of her more solemn sister, "the oh-so-serious woman." But when we think about the essence of the good-humor woman, we must begin with Mona Lisa.

MONA LISA WAS A GOOD-HUMOR WOMAN

In the first autumn of our marriage, Jeremy and I discovered Paris, and during the obligatory visit to the Louvre, I encountered Leonardo da Vinci's Mona Lisa. The painting was smaller than I expected, protected behind glass, and roped off like an E-ticket ride at Disneyland. Gazing over the heads of the crowd, I studied the smile that has captivated onlookers for almost 500 years.

Virtually everything about the Mona Lisa is in dispute —from who she was to why she was smiling—and the riddle of her identity has deepened with time. Various scholars have argued that her half-smile was the result of: a childhood case of palsy, the mourning of a mother who had lost a child, or her love affair with Leonardo. Different sources have suggested that she was Lisa Gherardini, the wife of Francesco del Giocondo, Isabella of Aragon, or Leonardo's mother, Caterina. Most recently, a computerized comparison at Bell Laboratories concluded that

Mona Lisa was actually a self-portrait of Leonardo himself.

Perhaps the most intriguing aspect of the Mona Lisa is the effect of her ineffable smile on the observer. This wonderfully admired painting has been stolen twice; copied on calendars, coasters, and cartoons; lampooned by *MAD* magazine and Gary Larson's *Far Side* comic strip, and been the subject of a song performed with memorable longing by Nat King Cole.

Men seem to respond to Mona Lisa's appearance, and women to her presence. Said one woman, "Her smile is the source of her power; what she knows, *I* want to know!" Said another, "Her attitude draws me to her even more than what she knows. She is approachable, powerful; I think I would enjoy talking to her."

What did Mona Lisa know? In a strict literal sense, we may never know. But as you master the art of lightening up, you can learn to convey your own powerful version of Mona Lisa's womanly strength and composure. For that reason—although Mona Lisa was clearly not a working woman—her compelling presence will preside as a muse to guide us through the pages that follow.

THE COURSE IN LIGHTENING UP

Because of your hard work, perseverance, and talent, you have earned the right to be taken seriously. As you continue reading, you will understand why being *too* serious can keep you from getting ahead, and how humor can be your secret weapon on your climb to the top. Throughout the book, you will find hundreds of anecdotes and inspiring examples of good-humored women, drawn from my consulting practice and my special seminars for women. In addition, you'll encounter both fictional and notable women who have learned to lighten up, including Geraldine Ferraro, Nora Charles in *The Thin Man* movies, and writer Lillian Hellman.

As you meet these smart and funny women, you'll find that their sense of humor is not a matter of zinging one-liners or being born to be glib; it is a state of mind, an *attitude* they have *learned* and practiced. Once learned, this attitude can make a remarkable difference in your self-esteem, in setting and approaching goals, handling relationships on the job, and keeping life in the office in manageable perspective.

The examples of good-humored women will be followed by step-by-step instructions and practice exercises that will enable you to develop the *perspective* and *skill* to use humor as a strategy to create less stress and more success on the job. You will become familiar with a series of special techniques for using humor as a professional tool, including "mirroring," "situation comedy," "comic comparison," "the art of being at ease," and "the MBA formula."

As you practice these techniques, you will learn:

- How to use humor as a communication tool with even the surliest co-worker or most demanding client.

- How to apply the skill of "silent comedy" to change your response to stressful events— anything from an unexpected deadline to a computer snafu.

- How to stop worrying about remembering the punchline, by using five sure-fire humor formulas.

- How lightening up can lessen your fear of taking risks, making mistakes, or being wrong.

- How to get "in on the joke" with men in the office–without imitating male humor.

- How a sense of humor can skewer sexism.

- How to bring laughter home to friends, lovers, and family.

As a good-humor woman, you can take yourself seriously without losing your playful side. You will understand how laughter is the best revenge, since humor maps the road beyond job frustration and disappointment. Laughter provides the grand alternative to feeling angry, depressed, or defensive. When you lighten up, "getting even" means that you control the emotional climate in your office and restore the balance of power in your favor.

As you read, I trust that you will experiment with techniques and ideas that will nurture your unique sense of humor and enhance your sense of pride and joy in doing your job. And as you turn these pages, I hope that your home and your office will be filled with the wonderful sound of your laughter.

CHAPTER TWO

....

THE OH-SO-
SERIOUS WOMAN

THE OH-SO-SERIOUS WOMAN: THREE DEFINITIONS

Jane S., 29, a stockbroker, describes her as "the kind of woman who trips on her high heels as she walks down the street and then turns around to see who or what tripped her."

Says Carla O., 41, an attorney, "She's the one who tries to make every report read like a college English paper. She takes longer than everyone else in the office to finish her work."

Sarah T., 38, a senior manager, suggests, "This is the woman who can't succeed as a manager—she is so preoccupied with the details that she misses the big picture."

D o you recognize this woman? Are you busy fussing with your hair, crossing your ankles, agonizing over details, collecting sexist slights? If you are watching your every move, your high standards will exact a high price. But seriously folks, in this chapter you will discover that your self-absorption is not only stressful but also creates roadblocks in your career path and prevents you from feeling pride and joy about your work.

The art of lightening up on the job is not simply a laughing matter; it's a brand-new set of dance steps. Consider some questions that offer clues to the kinds of beliefs and behaviors that can keep you from reaching your potential.

DISCOVERY QUIZ

DOES BEING TOO SERIOUS KEEP YOU FROM SUCCEEDING?

1. *Do you believe that laughter is the best medicine—but you don't know where to pick up your prescription?*

2. *Do you think that a sense of humor is something you are born with?*

3. *Do you think good humor means telling jokes—and you can never remember the punchline?*

4. *When you make a mistake, do you make excuses, cry, berate yourself, expect the worst catastrophe?*

5. *Do you try to camouflage your feminine or distinct personality traits by dressing primly, keeping your office devoid of personal touches?*

6. *Do you think people who have fun on the job don't get the job done?*

....

7. *Do you think that humor is just for the staff around the water cooler, and that being a manager is all serious business?*

8. *Do you feel uncomfortable with men's humor in the office?*

9. *Do you smolder with resentment whenever a man makes a patronizing remark?*

10. *Do you reserve your good humor for the job— and your foul temper for family and friends at home?*

EXPLORE YOUR ANSWERS:

1. If you answered "yes," take special note of Chapter 3's description of how humor reduces stress.

2. If "yes," you'll be intrigued with Chapter 4's discussion of humor as a state of mind.

3. If "yes," see Chapter 5's plan for five sure-fire humor formulas.

4 & 5. If "yes" to either or both, you will welcome Chapter 6's instruction in "The Art of Being at Ease."

6 & 7. If "yes" to either or both, you'll enjoy learning about humor as a management tool in Chapter 7.

8. If "yes," practice techniques for getting in on the joke—without imitating men's humor— in Chapter 8.

9. If "yes," take a closer look at how mirth can work to dissolve sexual tension on the job in Chapter 9.

10. If "yes," Chapters 10 and 11 will help you carry your sense of lightness into your life after work.

The Successful Woman: Four Mistaken Beliefs

Why are you shaking your head? You say that you're serious about having a rewarding career, and when I say lighten up, you think of being seen as a "lightweight"? Maybe it's time to reconsider some of your beliefs about successful women.

BELIEF #1: SHE CAN'T RISK BEING FUNNY (OR SHE WON'T BE TAKEN SERIOUSLY)

So you've decided not to laugh on the outside. I'll bet your thoughts mirror those of Carol S., 29, a bright young engineer. "Sometimes, when I get a new client, I can tell by the way he looks at me that he's wondering why I'm not a man and ten years older. I'd *never* joke during our meeting since I plan to show him I am twenty times better than any man in my position."

Carol's concern about her credibility will undoubtedly cause her to present herself in a tense, humorless way. Her formality conveys a lack of confidence and keeps her from establishing rapport with her client. In fact, she will never establish a strong presence unless she acts—in just one respect—like the man the client might have preferred. *That* man would be assured enough of his competence to be light, to joke.

Compare Carol's timid approach with Ellen J.'s. Ellen is a 32-year-old computer sales representative who had repeatedly failed to get a crucial meeting with a company vice president. When she asked him to lunch, he said he didn't take time to go to lunch. Still she persisted, "Okay, I'll bring the bread, cheese, and ants and we'll have a picnic at your desk." He laughed and set up an appointment for the following week.

Women like Ellen demonstrate their confidence by using humor to persuade and motivate. Barbara T., 46, a top state administrator, took a similar light approach in the early days of her appointment to a male-dominated department. "I made a point of not coming on like a young barracuda; I used humor to gain their trust, to draw them into the situation. Now, they respect my ability, but that came later."

Let's set the record straight: A woman can be funny and still maintain her credibility. The research cited in Chapter 1 suggests, paradoxically, that a woman *must* be funny in order to be taken seriously. In the Hall and Associates study where 84 percent of personnel executives said people with a sense of humor did a better job, employees with a sense of humor were viewed as more flexible, creative, and adaptable to change—all qualities related to humor as a state of mind.

In Chapters 4 and 5, you'll learn how to extend your sense of lightness beyond simply laughing at other people's jokes. Susan B., 32, is an architect who has grown into her own delicious sense of humor. She says, "Humor is the thing that comes with being confident. I don't have to be macho to be confident; I could even wear silly clothes. With humor, it's off with the gray suit and on with the clown suit."

BELIEF #2: SHE STRIVES FOR PERFECTION (SHE CAN'T AFFORD TO BE WRONG)

Diana R., a 33-year-old CPA, once allowed a single pearl

button to sabotage her success. She was in the middle of delivering a well-prepared, lively talk to a group of accountants about setting up a private practice. As she glanced down at her notes, she noticed one of the buttons on her blue silk shirt was unfastened. At that moment, her concentration shifted from her subject matter. She was unable to stop thinking: "How long has it been unbuttoned? Should I excuse myself? What if they think I'm being provocative?" Admits Diana, "I ended up blowing the presentation."

While it is easy enough for us to imagine Diana fastening the errant button as she continued to talk, her paralysis is typical of women who strive to appear letter-perfect in their presentation of themselves. Captured by the smallest detail, Diana lost sight of the bigger picture; her self-absorption destroyed her effectiveness. Contrast Diana's response with that of Dee R., 28, a data processing manager, when she discovered her unbuttoned state; she quickly fastened the button and commented; "Ah, my trick blouse."

Observe the approach of Nora M., a 40-year-old broker, to her recent error. She had planned to show a group of clients a slide presentation featuring several urban commercial properties. After three slides of oceanfront lots appeared on the screen, it was obvious she had brought the wrong carousel. As the room grew quiet, all eyes focused on Nora, who responded by casting her eyes skyward and borrowing a line from TV's "Star Trek": "Beam me up, Scotty." While the group laughed, she hurried down the hall to locate the correct carousel.

In her light-handed response, Nora was able to acknowledge her mistake and to joke about her awkward predicament. She did both without resorting to a Joan Rivers "I-was-clumsy-as-a child" routine. When she made fun of the *situation* rather than *herself,* her grace under pressure conveyed confidence and credibility.

"I spent ten years trying to be perfect," explains Lynn B., 43, a stockbroker, recalling the morning she had ridden a car ferry to work and walked off, leaving her car to travel back home without her. She realized her mistake at about 10:30 and took several hours off to recover her car. When she returned to the office, a male colleague greeted her warmly, saying, "I'm so glad to find out that you aren't perfect." "I had to laugh," admits Lynn. "His comment was the start of a wonderful friendship in the office, one I hadn't been open to in the past."

When you see your mistakes in bold print, as if somehow your errors cost the company more than those of your colleagues, you'll suffer from fear of trying. Paralyzed by the thought of being wrong, you will be unable to take risks, create alliances, gamble on hunches, or suggest bold ideas—to do the very things that will make you shine in your workplace. In addition, your perfectionism puts other people on the defensive and the offensive. They'll be on the lookout to catch you in a potential slip. It's a crazy circle; you can't relax, they can't relax.

The search for perfection is the nagging companion to the belief that women must be "20 times better than a man" in her position. When you defend or deny the errors that men kid one another about, you bear an uncanny resemblance to the much-maligned woman who "takes things too personally."

"When I make a mistake," says Gloria M., 44, a city manager, "I don't make excuses or belittle myself; I just acknowledge my error or joke about it. It's my way of saying, 'This time me, next time you.' " In Chapter 6, you'll discover guidelines and examples of how you can remain credible amidst a comedy of your errors.

BELIEF #3: SHE MUST HIDE HER "FEMININE SIDE"

Denise L., 31, an insurance broker, stopped in a wine shop to buy champagne for a friend's birthday dinner. Dressed in her usual weekend attire—leather pants, punkish ankle boots, hair tied in a ponytail—she ran into her biggest client. "I felt my face turn bright red," she recalls. "He seemed to be staring at my shoes, and we had this horrible, stilted conversation."

Denise's embarrassment at being seen undressed for success mirrors the kind of advice we have been hearing for years. Being serious about work meant that a woman needed to hide her "feminine side." This included legs, laughter, family life, feelings. Maintaining a professional profile meant submerging our personal style, and clothes were symbolic of that camouflage. "Women were seen as emotional creatures," one banker explains. "If we wanted to be treated equally, we thought we should stifle all human emotions and wear blouses buttoned up to our upper lips."

One by one, good-humored women have come out of hiding. "I got tired of falling back asleep when I opened my closet in the morning," says Janet R., 27, an attorney. "I feel confident enough to wear whatever I like. If a client can't handle my fuchsia shirt, that's his problem." Angela M., 39, an entrepreneur, remembers a similar turning point: "One day I put on a boring camel-hair suit and decided to pair it with a pink reptile tie. It was time for me to send a different message to my clients. I wanted to tell them: 'We can get the job done for you and still laugh a little.' "

But the larger issue isn't clothes, it is how you express yourself. "I succeed more when I stop trying so hard," comments one executive. As you lighten up, you will refuse to be a woman in gray; you may even decide to donate those Minnie Mouse ties to Disneyland. More important, you will stop hiding the wonderful qualities traditionally attributed to women: warmth, compassion, and empathy. "I get further with a client by being at ease with myself," says Anita R., a 25-year-old architect.

In Chapter 6, you'll encounter lightness as the art of being at ease and learn from the experiences of women like Rebecca M., a 41-year-old corporate consultant who explains, "My success as a consultant depends on interviewing top executives so I can understand the culture of each company I work with. I find executives—both men and women—respond to my (traditionally female) empathic approach to them. Because I am at ease with this softer quality in myself, I am able to get the 'hard' facts I need from them. So many times after I present a management seminar, I will hear this gratifying question: 'How did you ever learn so much about our company?' "

BELIEF #4: SHE ALWAYS ATTACKS SEXISM (SHE MUST BE ON GUARD)

In the judge's chambers, the 50-year-old male prosecutor had just called Miriam J., a 29-year-old defense attorney, "my dear" for the third—and last—time. "I'm *not* your dear," snapped Miriam, and then listened in horror while the offending gentleman delivered a windy speech assuring her that: (a) he was sorry, (b) he wasn't a chauvinist, and (c) he had a daughter of his own. "He totally distracted the judge from the case I was trying to build," recalls Miriam. "I won the battle, but I lost the war."

Another attorney, Julie B., 34, spent the morning with a male colleague and a new client who addressed her as "young lady." Her male colleague grew increasingly uncomfortable and whispered audibly to Julie, "Are you going to let him get away with that?" "Why not?" asked the confident Ms. B. "At my age, it's a compliment."

Like Miriam and Julie, we are all learning to choose our battles more carefully. "You can't exactly work the phrase 'sexist pig' into the conversation," says one personnel director. "I don't respond to every chauvinist comment," explains a savvy county official. "If a man asks me about my love life, he's just trying to get a rise out of me and I refuse to take *him* seriously."

As a successful woman, you can be freer to stop personalizing a man's patronizing comments. He probably says the same thing to all of the "girls." You decide: Is your valuable time best spent on a mission to change his vocabulary, or to get the job done? In Chapter 9 we'll talk about how to separate the serious situation of sexual harassment from sexual heckling—a situation that can be managed with humor.

Leslie M., 39, an engineer, has learned to choose her battles. In a recent staff meeting she found herself taking notes while her male colleague outlined the strategy she had prepared with him. "In the past, I would have fumed about his assumption that a woman would take notes. But I took the notes; because I don't have to prove myself every time. If he does it again, I'll stop him."

As a confident woman, you can allow yourself to stop generalizing about men. "I've stopped seeing every chauvinistic remark or act as standing for a void in society," explains Donna C., a 43-year-old training consultant, who relishes telling the tale of a recent corporate seminar she presented: "I was gesturing broadly to make a point when one of the men grabbed my hand and kissed it. The room inhaled; but I ignored him, kept talking, didn't miss a beat. Afterward, several men apologized to me, saying, 'I hope you don't think all of the men in our company are like that.' " In Chapter 8 you'll learn to respond to this kind of male humor—often cruel and aggressive—without imitating it.

BUT CAN *I* LEARN TO BE FUNNY?

I was sitting next to a cherubic young girl on a downtown bus when a man across the aisle asked her age. She held up four fingers and he shouted, "What's the matter, can't you talk?" This little darling giggled and answered, "What's the matter, can't you *see*?" As I watched, I thought about how few women are gifted with her instinctive good humor. At the age when Lily Tomlin had her classmates snickering in the lunchroom, most of us were fretting about our homework.

I admit that few of us have the bratty, funny instincts of this four-year-old. We tend to suffer from what the French call the wit of the staircase: thinking of brilliant lines after the fact—on the subway platform or going upstairs to bed. But remember, the ability to lighten up is a state of mind. The process of becoming a good-humor woman is less of offering a snappy comeback (although I've got some choice laugh lines for you to borrow) and more of appreciating life's lighter side.

What are you waiting for? As you lighten up, you can jettison painful, self-conscious feelings and express your special style. As a good-humor woman, your fuse will glow longer; you'll be less angry, defensive, tearful—slower to blame and willing to look for your own participation in the problem. Your lighter touch will allow you to defuse explosive feelings and convey authority in awkward moments. Most important, you'll be able to accept your foibles and setbacks with a bemused grace. Says Paula G., 43, a top-level manager, "Whenever I make a mistake, I picture myself as Mae West, saying 'Ohhh, I used to be like Snow White, but then I drifted.' "

Your ability to lighten up will sharpen your perspective about painful events, professional challenges and setbacks, taking you beyond memorable one-liners or cosmic giggles. Perhaps your experience will be like one of these two:

> Maria M., 30, spent a bitter, ruminative summer following her forced resignation as an executive in a major record company. Brooding over her long list of sexist encounters, she considered a lawsuit. But instead, she began lunching with industry contacts and looking for another position. Says Maria: "If I sued them, it would cost tons of money and years of living with my anger. Looking back now, I see the role of chauvinism, but I also see my naiveté— thinking that doing a great job would be enough—prevented me from being more effective. *I took it so personally; but now I see it as a game, and I think I'll be one hell of a player this time.*"

> Three years ago, Erika B., 34, was a driven commercial real estate broker whose determination to succeed caused her to view every business meeting as a "life-or-death situation." She laughs softly when she describes the move into her own business where she practiced "being serious, without turning everything into a funeral." Her sense of lightness is exhilarating: "I still try to achieve my best; but the

difference is that I have learned to value the process, to value what I learned from *not* getting what I want. These days I may get less; but I have more fun getting it."

As you read the three chapters of the next section, you'll enjoy a bird's-eye view of how humor works, explore your good humor as a state of mind, and practice five sure-fire formulas to express your unique sense of humor.

And so the answer is yes; you *can* learn to be a good-humored woman, starting right now.

PART TWO

A QUICK CRASH COURSE
IN LIGHTENING UP

CHAPTER THREE

....

HOW
MIRTH WORKS

*L*isten to two amusing stories. Each illustrates one of the essential ways that mirth can work for you: first, as a communication tool, and next, as a technique to manage stress. Notice how each of these good-humored women responded to a difficult situation with humor and reduced its negative impact.

Laura G., 34, a management consultant, had just completed a management audit for an important new client, a prestigious high-tech firm. As she prepared for her first meeting with the newly appointed CEO, she found that she had only negative data to report. She began her meeting with the executive by asking, "Do you want the good news or the bad first?" When he replied "The good, of course," she responded, "The good news is: No one blames you!" He laughed and said, "Now tell me about the bad news."

Laura's sense of humor allowed her to communicate a lighter outlook, and she was able to defuse the loaded situation and begin to establish a rapport with her new client.

Carolyn M., 31, a small-business owner, approached the podium to address a large professional audience. As she ascended the platform stairs, she tripped and landed flat on her back. She then stood up, stepped to the microphone, and said, "My entrance reminds me of my business: a quick start, a rapid fall, and a fast recovery."

Carolyn's sense of humor allowed her to refocus a potentially humiliating situation and reduce its stressful impact–while maintaining her professional profile.

HOW HUMOR COMMUNICATES

In this chapter, you'll explore the ways in which humor can enhance your job performance by enriching communication skills and increasing your capacity to manage stress. Let's begin with a closer look at three ways you might use humor to communicate.

HUMOR CONVEYS AUTHORITY

Your sense of humor offers a powerful means of establishing and maintaining your authority. Suppose that you are presiding over a marketing meeting for your department when a late-arriving man announces loudly, "I only came to this meeting because you are so pretty." (Sound familiar?) Before you ask him whether he's had charisma bypass surgery, choose your most powerful ploy.

DO YOU SAY:

A. "I'm chairing this meeting because I have the highest sales figures for the third quarter."

B. "This isn't a beauty pageant; it's a marketing meeting."

C. "Then you should be *pretty* interested in what I have to say."

Let's contrast the three potential responses.

A. is a *defensive* response. You don't need to justify your leadership role. When you list your credentials, you accept the latecomer's definition of the situation—your sole qualification is your silky lashes—instead of defining the situation in your own terms. With this defensive response, you lose control of the moment and maybe, the meeting. But tell me, why are you taking his absurd remark so seriously?

Your colleagues might laugh at *aggressive* remark B., but it is a poorly aimed shot, one that focuses even more attention on your appearance. Besides, your anger may make him defensive and the situation could quickly deteriorate into some nasty, dueling banter.

C., a *mirthful* response, confirms your authority by making light of the situation without humiliating him. Your sense of humor enhances your credibility with the message: "I know I'm in charge here, and your comments don't change a thing."

Communications experts would view this interaction as a power struggle about who defines the moment. If you use humor to make fun of the *situation*, rather than to defend yourself or attack your "complimentary" co-worker, you will shift the balance of power in your favor and maintain control of the meeting.

HUMOR PROVIDES FEEDBACK AND BUILDS RAPPORT

As you share your sense of humor with clients and colleagues, you'll gain important feedback about how to form a strong working alliance with them. For example, Connie M., 41, a commercial real estate broker, finds that her lightness can reward her with needed information from a prospective client. Recently she met with the owner of a prestigious new office high-rise whose answers to her questions made Harpo Marx seem talkative. After asking him the same question in three different ways, she tried a humorous approach: "Henry, I play a lot of poker, and I'm not going to be able to read your cards if you hold them so close to your chest." He laughed, answered her question directly, and eventually agreed to name Connie the leasing agent for the building.

With other clients, a lighter approach can offer information about their personality and working style. In some cases, you may learn the essential fact that the client lacks a sense of humor. Explains Mary C., 29, a banking executive, "My sense of humor is the way I can get my toe in the water with a client. I use my sense of humor to gauge their response, to see how they react. I look for a reciprocal response—and if I get a blank stare, I change track and find a better way to approach them."

Rhonda G., 36, a food services executive, recalls a memorable new job where her lighter touch was the key to establishing rapport with Gayle P., her angry new administrative assistant. Her assistant's anger was not without cause: Gayle was 10 years older than Rhonda, had worked for the company five years longer, and had expected to be promoted to Rhonda's new job. At the beginning of their first meeting, Rhonda acknowledged the situation by saying, "I'm the new kid on the block here and I've got lots to learn. But I've heard you have a great sense of humor. So let's go out to lunch and laugh, and I'll get your views on this department."

When the two returned from lunch, Gayle turned to a co-worker, saying, "Maybe this will work out after all; Rhonda really has a wonderful sense of humor."

HUMOR DEFUSES CONFLICT

Although some situations call for a Superpower Summit, on many other occasions humor can make a powerful point and hasten changed behavior–without a heated conversation. For example: Deborah L., 32, a nurse, was furious with a young resident who was in the habit of tossing a patient's chart in her direction after reading it– often without warning. Instead of an angry confrontation, she was determined to make fun of the situation. The next time a chart flew in her direction, she ducked and exclaimed, "Hit the deck!" Her approach was right on target: everyone laughed, including the resident, whose charts never sailed again.

Humor lets you speak about the unspeakable and allows you to navigate successfully through ticklish situations. Hannah R., 37, is an accountant who planned to lunch with a valued client whose bill was almost a year overdue. Her opener, after the coffee was served: "Ed, you are an important client of our firm, but your bill is long overdue. We've carried you longer than your mother did!" As a result, they worked out a plan for payment.

I applaud the savvy, funny solution of a group of managers who were outraged about the antics of the office voyeur who frequently "dropped" his pen under the conference table and then enjoyed the view while he retrieved it. After the women banded together, his last sneaky peek took place when he was greeted under the table by seven kneecaps inked to spell out the message, "HI STEVE."

Imagine that you are on the phone with a customer who has an angry inquiry about her account or bill. The customer is impatient, your computer is sluggish, and you know it will take at least five minutes to retrieve the needed information. How can you keep the customer on the line—without her twisting in the wind? Evaluate three choices.

WOULD YOU SAY:

A. "It's not my fault. My computer is just slow. I'm doing the best I can."

B. "Keep your powder dry. This is going to take some time."

C. "Do you have your lunch? I have mine. Why don't we both eat while we wait for my computer to respond? It looks like it's going to be a while."

I'd avoid A.; your *defensive* response will fuel her impatience. Ditto B.; an *aggressive* answer will up the ante and may provoke a fresh volley of anger. Stick with C., a *mirthful* reply, one that makes fun of the frustrating situation, will lower her blood pressure and allow you to maintain your composure.

In later chapters, you'll have ample opportunity to take a lighter view of your own communication skills on the job. Now let's take a moment to ponder the impossibility of laughing and carrying a heavy suitcase at the same time. In other words, here's how humor can relieve the stresses of life in the office.

*S*HE *W*HO *L*AUGHS, *L*ASTS: *T*HREE *W*AYS *H*UMOR *R*ELIEVES *S*TRESS

Before the apple, Eve had no sense of humor. Neither did Adam. There was no need for humor in the Garden of Eden—no tension, no stress, no cause for criticism or alarm. We might picture the first lovers smiling with pleasure, but not with comic relief. But after their fall from grace, and especially after the birth of sons Cain and Abel, we can imagine the need for humor. As our commitments multiplied throughout the ages—amid the daily clamor of jobs, unpaid bills, dirty laundry, and love something short of paradise—we have developed humor as an instant stress reliever. You can put it to work for you in a number of ways.

HUMOR RELABELS STRESS

My friend Nancy works as an aide to a congressman whose vote on Contra aid once made him a target of a major demonstration in his local office. When I called Nancy that evening after what I assumed would be a very stressful time for her, she described the day as having been "hilarious." "Hilarious?" I asked. "How could a demonstration against your boss be funny?" Nancy's explanation: "I'm a child of the sixties, and you can't imagine demonstrations in the eighties! The leader of the group called me at seven-thirty this morning and said, 'We'd like to demonstrate; what time would be *convenient* for the congressman?' "

Was her day stressful? Absolutely. Did her humor make a difference in how she managed and listened to the demonstrators? No question. Her ability to stand back and see the humor as well as the seriousness of the occasion helped her to maintain her cool in the heated discussion of opinion. Nancy's response suggests that stress lies not simply in events, but in how we *label* or *interpret* those events.

To understand stress as a labeling process, simply contrast the characters of Frank Burns and Hawkeye on the television series "M*A*S*H." In the midst of stressful events, Frank Burns was always whining and complaining while Hawkeye was pointing to a sly, funny side of the crisis. Anne G., 39, a marketing rep, offers this explanation: "Being too serious about problems at work gave me headaches. I finally realized that sometimes circumstances can't change; but my approach to them can change—by the way I look at them."

Any stressful event—your supervisor's unexpected demand, a colleague's patronizing remark, a meeting with a less-than-charming customer—has the potential to set off a chain of physical changes including muscle tension, rapid breathing, and an increased flow of adrenaline to your bloodstream. But how you *label* a stressful event determines whether these changes take place.

In the midst of a stressful encounter, do you find yourself grinding your teeth, thinking, "Who does she think she is?" or "Why does this always happen to me?" Or do you relabel a stressful scenario with a more humorous touch (as Nancy or Hawkeye might do) by mentally noting, "This moment is strictly loony tunes," or "This client belong in the annals of *Ripley's Believe It or Not.*"

In the next chapter, through the practice of "silent comedy," you'll learn to label stressful moments with a humorous eye and telegraph a different set of messages to your brain. The results of your laughter and mirthful outlook will stimulate your cardiovascular system, resulting in deep muscle relaxation and the release of endorphins—

our body's natural pain-killers. Here laughter earns its reputation as the best medicine. In his book *Anatomy of an Illness*, Norman Cousins called laughter "a bulletproof vest that protects you against the ravages of negative emotions."

Cousins speaks from experience: After doctors emphasized the hopelessness of his condition, he battled a progressive disease of the spine with a treatment regimen of massive doses of vitamin C and regularly scheduled comic interludes of old "Candid Camera" episodes and Marx Brothers movies. Ten minutes of belly laughs afforded several hours of painless sleep.

LIGHTNESS PUTS PROBLEMS IN PERSPECTIVE

"One night, I was at home crying my eyes out," recalls Sherry B. "Here I am, boo-hoo-hooing about a disappointment on the job; I reach for another Kleenex to blow my nose and I notice the box is empty. I search everywhere, only to discover that I am also out of toilet paper. But by then, I couldn't stop laughing. Laughter is a daily reminder that life goes on—even when you are hysterical—Kleenex doesn't magically disappear."

With a lightened perspective, you don't have to wait until "someday" to laugh about today's problems; you can begin immediately to view them from a healing distance.

Your sense of lightness can put people and problems in a manageable perspective, one that allows you (as my father used to say) "to keep your brain in neutral" and to maintain your concentration and professionalism. This means that you can be light without laughing out loud. Here your comic perspective becomes a more cosmic one because you see problems as time limited or being only a small part of the bigger picture.

Imagine yourself sitting in your office; phones jangling, nerves frazzled, embroiled in an encounter with a snarling client or kvetching co-worker. Or picture your-self seated in a restaurant across the table from a col-league who hasn't stopped whining since you sat down. Quick–before you suggest that he add more fiber to his diet–you might share the thoughts of one of these women:

> Kristin C., 33, a banker: "Whenever I get stuck in an unbearable situation, I tell myself: 'I am not stuck here forever. This can only last as long as the duration of this (meeting, date, interview, phone call). Then I will leave and this moment will end–I'll get on with my life.' "

> Andrea R., 37, a college administrator: "When I get all tied up in a work snafu, the whole world seems to revolve around the problem. So I just look outside my window –at the sky, trees, pigeons. I instantly see the rest of life outside of my office and not just this lousy day."

> Randy G., 42, a marketing representa-tive: "Sometimes, when things are going badly, I just don't see any changes in my life. Then I try to picture myself as a pebble landing in the water. Maybe I can't see my own progress right now; but the pebble cre-ates ripples and eventually the ripples will reach the shore."

HUMOR DISTRACTS US FROM PAINFUL FEELINGS
"On the first day I did not think it was funny. I didn't think it was funny on the third day either, but I managed to

make a little joke about it," wrote Nora Ephron in *Heart-burn*, a thinly disguised novel about the pain Ephron felt when, in the seventh month of her pregnancy, she discovered her husband was having an affair. " 'The most unfair thing about this whole business,' I said, 'is that I can't even date.' I got a laugh on that though for all I know, my group was only laughing because they were trying to cheer me up. I needed cheering up."

Ephron was writing about a feeling we all recognize both on and off the job: when humor provides a momentary distraction from painful, angry, anxious feelings. Our sense of humor becomes the Scarlett O'Hara of our emotional life: We can think about the pain tomorrow. In the meantime, we summon the strength to confront the problem.

Freud wrote about using humor as a defense against pain and unpleasant reality, and his comments about joking are more useful than his misinformation about women. In *Jokes and Their Relation to the Unconscious*, he described humor as our "refusal to be hurt by the arrows of reality or be compelled to suffer. Humor insists that we are impervious to the wounds of the outside world and that these are merely occasions for our pleasure."

To put it another way: "The trick," said Peter O'Toole after he had doused a candle with his fingertips in a scene from *Lawrence of Arabia*, "is not to show that it hurts." Perhaps your use of humor as a pain-killer will be similar to Alice's or Brenda's.

> Alice C., 31, a software distributor, has learned to use humor to interrupt the flow of angry thoughts that "poison me." She remembers a recent client who phoned three days in a row and "received his entire education about software from me." Then,

he called to tell her he was buying from her competitor. "I was so angry after his phone call, I couldn't work for the rest of the morning," says Alice. "Then suddenly, I had a wonderful fantasy. I pictured myself going into Ernie's (his favorite restaurant) and writing on the wall of the women's room: 'For a good time call: (his name and office number).' I laughed out loud, went to lunch, and worked beautifully all afternoon."

Brenda L., 39, a training consultant, walked from backstage to the podium to present a management seminar to 600 executives. Suddenly, without warning, the audiovisual crew darkened the auditorium and shined an achingly bright light in her eyes. As Brenda recalls, "I couldn't even see the audience's faces. The light in my eyes was painful. I couldn't get the audience to laugh or respond; I knew I was bombing. But somehow I kept my composure and sense of control by thinking of myself as 'a deer caught in the headlights.' Later I told a friend, 'Now I know how Dan Quayle felt at his first press conference!' "

History informs us that Queen Elizabeth I relied on her court jester, Richard Tarlton, to distract her from the pain of her sovereign role. According to Doran, her biographer, jester Tarlton was able to tell Elizabeth more of her faults than her advisors and cure her melancholy better than any physician.

In the chapter that follows, you'll learn to become your own inner jester and cultivate humor as a state of mind. I predict that your own mirthful interludes will prevent you from engaging in the snarling repartee of some of Elizabeth's royal colleagues; for example, Queen Victoria: "We are *not* amused." Or worse, the Queen of Hearts: "Off with his head!"

CHAPTER FOUR

••

HUMOR AS A
STATE OF MIND

*H*umor is something I had to learn as an adult," explains Christine K., 45, a successful business consultant. "I grew up in a small family where everything was serious; my parents were completely devoid of humor. I was in my early thirties before I understood how to use humor. The lesson came in the form of my boss, Carol, who had a great dramatic sense of humor. By the time I left that job, I learned that I could be competent and still have a good time. I started to actively seek out people who were light, collected funny cartoons and cards, and learned to tell stories. Now, I take real pride in how well I've done at an emotional level, filling in the gaps of my up-bringing. I have really learned to not take everything so seriously."

Christine's success offers two lessons: how early experiences can nurture or deprive us of a sense of lightness; and also, that our past is not our destination. No matter what you learned as a child, you can, like Christine, become a woman of good humor.

The approach of this chapter will be to build on the giggles of girlhood to provide a basis for cultivating your sense of humor as *a state of mind*, an attitude that can shape the way you see the world. In the process of lightening up, this attitude comes first; before you can invite others to laugh out loud, you must develop the art of "silent comedy"—a powerful technique for laughing on the inside.

YOUR HUMOR PROFILE

What did you learn about laughing or expressing your point of view while sitting in the classroom or at the family dinner table? Let these recollections tickle your own memories:

> The nuns at her all-girls school told Patricia D. that she "used her hands too much." They forced her to keep her hands in her pockets when she talked.

> Deanne F.'s mother played practical jokes on her children and husband (rubber chicken on the pillow, plastic wrap on the toilet seat).

> Lee S. was sent to the principal's office for blurting out a joke that made kids laugh. Another time, she got sent into the hall when she couldn't stop giggling.

> Jodie A.'s dad had a warm, memorable laugh. When her parents had parties, she lay in bed and listened to his hearty laughter.

Next, use these questions to view your humor history.

DISCOVERY QUIZ

YOUR HUMOR HISTORY

1. What kinds of things did your mother and father laugh about: bathroom humor, practical jokes, sarcasm, puns, cartoons, formal jokes, stories?

2. Which TV or radio comedies were family favorites?

3. Who, if anyone, was the funniest person in your family?

4. Did your parents laugh at their mistakes? Did they make fun of themselves? Did they tease each other? Did they tease you? Was the banter affectionate or more aggressive?

5. Did your mother's/father's laugh sound most like: chuckling, giggling, snorting, cackling, wheezing, choking, hiccupping, belly-laughing?

6. Can you remember any funny schoolteachers? Any teachers who made fun of you? What kind of humor was it?

7. Did you have a friend in grade school or high school who often made you laugh?

8. Do you ever remember laughing so hard you couldn't stop? What did your parents or teachers do?

9. *Did a parent or teacher ever comment about the way you expressed yourself? About the sound of your laugh?*

10. *Do you remember telling jokes as a child?*

11. *What happened if you laughed at the "wrong time" at home, or at school?*

12. *Can you remember any "seed sentences" about laughter or humor that were planted in your mind by parents or teachers (for example, "A loud laugh betrays an empty mind")?*

EXPLORE YOUR ANSWERS:

What patterns do you see? Which people or events shaped or stifled your sense of humor? For example: did you grow up laughing at the earthy humor of "The Honeymooners," the angry brilliance of Lenny Bruce, the loopy antics of "I Love Lucy," or the perky angst of "Mary Tyler Moore"? What similarities and differences do you see between the humor (or lack of it) in your family circle and what amuses you today?

Once armed with a knowledge of the past, you can seek clues to your current sense of humor. To cultivate humor as a state of mind, you'll need the resources of past and present. Observe your present sense of humor for a few days. Remember that everyone is ticklish in different spots. Case in point: have you ever:

A. Watched a movie while everyone around you laughed except you?

B. Watched a movie and laughed, when you were the only one laughing?

Whether you answered yes to A. or B. or both, remember that one woman's chuckle is another woman's yawn. In the process of lightening up, you must discover and draw upon your unique sense of style and humor.

INCLUDE THESE QUESTIONS IN YOUR OBSERVATION:

How often do I laugh? Does my laugh sound different at work and home? Who are the colleagues or friends I laugh the most with; what qualities do they share in common? Which comedians make me laugh? Which film comedies get two thumbs up from me? Which cartoonists or comic strips show the world the way I see it?

PRACTICE

Study your sense of humor with the aid of a laughter log. You might, for example, sit down with the funny papers, read each strip, including "Prince Valiant," and see what you can learn about what tickles you. For example, do you find yourself chuckling at the arch, hip commentary of *Doonesbury* or the gentle jesting of *Peanuts*?

As you discover your particular brand of humor, you are ready to cultivate lightness as a state of mind. Beginning with the art of "silent comedy," you can work on relabeling stressful scenarios and developing an attitude that changes your reaction from high anxiety to high comedy.

THE ART OF SILENT COMEDY: THREE TECHNIQUES TO REDEFINE STRESSFUL EVENTS

With silent comedy, the humor is "all in your mind." Your laughter arises in pictures rather than words. You will use your imagination to relabel maddening, threatening situations. Notice how Jean A. used silent comedy to laugh at a problem situation—and prepared to do battle with it.

> Jean A., 45, an advertising executive, had just completed what she thought was a brilliant campaign presentation to a client. But when she called for questions, she was greeted by silence. She recalls, "My stomach started churning and I had this frozen smile on my face, when suddenly I had the funniest image: I thought about how the 'Saturday Night Live' cameras used to scan the audience and focus on a face with a quirky caption underneath. I pictured myself on 'SNL' with a caption under my face saying, 'She once gave a client presentation and no one asked a question!' The image amused and relaxed me and I was able to wait more confidently for the discussion to take off."

To practice the art of silent comedy, try to rethink your situation in one of three ways.

PUT ON A FUNNY HAT

Take time out from a trying situation to enjoy *a comic image of yourself.* You can do this by asking: "What does this situation remind me of?" For example:

- Did you just say yes to overtime, an extra committee meeting, dinner with an out-of-town client?

  Picture yourself with a halo and wings, or imagine the ceremony in which you are elevated to sainthood.

- Are you surrounded by papers, pressures, deadlines, calls to return?

  Picture yourself as a duck: calm on the surface, but paddling like hell underneath the water.

- Stuck in a boring meeting? No need to grit your teeth or sigh loudly.

  Picture yourself as a pulp mystery writer capturing the meeting on paper. Write on your notes, "It was a dark and stormy night..."

Each of your mental images provides a humor break (one more refreshing than coffee or Valium) and allows you to return to the situation with composure and concentration.

FOLLOW ART LINKLETTER'S ADVICE

Let's reconsider Art Linkletter's classic corny version of silent comedy. Said he, "When you are nervous, picture the other person naked." There's a shadow of a good idea here; when you *picture a good-humored image of a difficult person*, you have a powerful means of mastering a stressful situation. Listen to Bobby R., 30, a marketing specialist who was abruptly fired by her patronizing, overbearing boss. "I was determined to stay light and keep myself from crying," recalls Bobby, "so when I looked at him, I pictured him as a Mafia godfather–ordering me cut out of the action." Practice changing your picture of problem people:

- Fed up with the office gossip?

  Picture him or her as the subject of a revealing, shocking story on the front page of *The National Inquirer*–complete with unflattering pictures.

- Bored with your prissy colleague?

  Picture her at Woodstock or having mistakenly wandered into an X-rated film festival.

- Can't cope with an obnoxious client or overbearing boss?

  Picture the person on the beach looking flabby in a swimsuit or seated at the "kids' table" for a holiday dinner.

Each comic image allows you to keep less-than-charming people at arm's length. By changing your view, you can keep them from controlling your behavior.

ASK A BARBARA WALTERS QUESTION
Ms. Walters is an astute interviewer with a fine sense of lightness, and she has a penchant for the kind of question

I find amusing. I call these queries her "If you were a tree, what tree would you be?" questions. Each question evokes a *comic comparison,* one that allows you to see the absurd along with the serious. Practice these playful questions:

- Which novel best describes this year's budget? (*Crime and Punishment, Jaws, Gone with the Wind*)

- Which music should be playing as you attempt to meet a hair-pulling deadline? (*"The Impossible Dream," "Climb Every Mountain," "Flight of the Bumblebee"*)

- Your new boss—the one from corporate in Chicago—reminds you of which film character? (Darth Vader, E. T., RoboCop)

When you practice these three silent comedy routines, you can express your sense of humor without saying a word. And the beauty of silent comedy is that it takes place in the playground of your mind. The next step on the road to lightness will be sharing what you see.

SHOW AND TELL

The "show and tell" technique of silent comedy involves pausing in the middle of a maddening or stressful situation to think of someone to tell about the incident. This allows you to view your problems and pressures from what Darlene R., 34, an editor, calls "a front seat at the movies." As she elaborates, "The more I can step outside and watch things happen, the more I can see the comic side of life. Everything becomes an interesting story to tell a friend later on."

For me, show and tell has become a four-star technique for maintaining a humorous state of mind. For example, the time last spring, at the end of an exhausting lecture tour, when my alarm sounded in a hotel room in Hartford, Connecticut. I sprang into action: called room service for coffee, donned a pair of sweats, and headed down the hall for a bucket of ice to apply to my face (a little wake-up tip I had learned from Joan Crawford while reading *Mommie Dearest*). When I returned to my room and tried the key in the lock, I couldn't budge the door—I had accidentally lodged the closet door behind my front door.

As I stood pushing on the door, I felt the rising tension; my face reddened, muscles tensed, my thoughts raced: "I'm going to be late to my talk, I'll miss my plane and my friend's birthday party in Seattle tonight." Then suddenly I thought about telling the story to Jeremy when he picked me up at the airport, and I started to laugh. As I relaxed, the wire hanger I was using to dislodge the closet door (another Joan Crawford tip) caught hold and the door swung open.

You can begin to practice the show and tell technique immediately. List the most stressful or frustrating moments of the past week. Who could have shared the story with you? Who are the people who appreciate the aggravations and absurdities of your life? Keep those folks in mind during your most troubling times.

The next time you find yourself in a stressful snafu, STOP! Take a deep breath and imagine yourself saying to a friend or lover, "You're not going to believe this," or "I saved this one just for you." Picture his or her face: smiling, laughing with you, helping you to gain perspective on the problem at hand. With show and tell, you discover the meaning of comic relief.

DEVELOPING A "THEORY OF RELATIVITY": TWO TECHNIQUES TO TURN THE LIGHTS ON

If Einstein's challenge was to convince his fellow physicists that absolutes did not exist, your task is to develop a theory of relativity to apply to the people and events in your life. Whatever the pressures of the moment—a computer failure, a project delay, a sniping co-worker—you can learn to lighten up and gain distance and perspective on the problem. Don't feel sheepish if your theory of relativity sounds clichéd; remember, you are the only one watching or listening, and your tried-and-truism may be just the trick to turn the lights on. Try the following two techniques.

PAINT A DIFFERENT PICTURE

You've reached a stalemate: your boss is pressuring you to cut your operating budget again, a colleague makes decisions without consulting you, the client has some reservations about your bright ideas. Take a moment and entertain a different image of your situation.

- Picture yourself placing your problem inside a pale, yellow balloon, letting it go, watching it drift until it is a tiny pastel dot in the sky.

- Instead of picturing your boss or colleague as moving farther and farther away from you, imagine that you are both magnets—drawn irresistibly to each other's ideas.

- Picture your problem as a giant rock that stands in your way. Envision that rock getting smaller and smaller until it becomes a tiny pebble that you simply kick aside.

As you immerse yourself in these images, your perspective changes and you create a more comfortable distance from which to consider the problem.

CHOOSE A LARGER FRAME

You and a co-worker have had a series of skirmishes about small but loaded issues. She uses your computer time, "forgets" to return a file, interrupts you during meetings. Pause and look at a bigger picture.

- Ask yourself: 10 years from now, how important will this problem be?

- Imagine complaining to your great-great granddaughter about your co-worker's misbehavior.

- Picture yourself presenting your complaints in a courtroom before a full jury.

- Try to remember what you were frustrated about on the job at precisely this moment two weeks ago. (You can't remember, can you?)

With practice, these playful images will keep the big picture in focus and you'll be able to view problems less emotionally, in a more "relative" perspective.

Television reporter Diane Sawyer has clearly cultivated humor as a state of mind. In a recent speech, she told a story that detailed her use of "silent comedy," "show and tell," as well as an amusing "theory of relativity." She described the first night of a "60 Minutes" assignment in Afghanistan: She retired to her tent and as she climbed into her sleeping bag, she felt bugs the size of Buicks crawling all over her body. Determined to be a good sport and not complain, she put on an additional layer of clothing, wrapped it close to her skin with dental floss, and tied two tampons together to cover her eyes. Sawyer recalled that she fell asleep thinking, "I can't *wait* until someone tells me I have a *glamorous* job!"

As Sawyer suggests, using humor as a state of mind is a private matter; it's allowing your thoughts to be as outrageous as you please—because no one is listening. When you have practiced this mirthful point of view, you'll be ready to experiment with the five sure-fire humor formulas in the next chapter. It's time to start laughing out loud.

CHAPTER FIVE

HUMOR
101

*E*lizabeth B., 36, a principal in an architecture firm, was frustrated with the slow decision making of David G., one of her partners. She knew David had a good sense of humor, so she sent him a cartoon and a note to open the discussion. The cartoon pictured two women outside a pie shop: one woman was saying, "Let's go in and buy a chocolate cream pie"; the other replied, "Let's just go in and see what happens." Elizabeth enclosed a memo that said, "This cartoon reminds me of our meeting on Tuesday." David called after receiving the cartoon, and the two met and were able to take a fresh approach to their stalemated process.

Elizabeth's light touch reminds us that bringing a sense of humor into the office is not a matter of telling jokes or of being born with a silver tongue. Much of your mirth at work involves taking time to plan for a lighter approach. After last chapter's practice of sharing silent comedy with a close friend, I know you'll enjoy experimenting with the five sure-fire humor formulas in this chapter. As you practice using these formulas, you'll be able to use humor to make a point, elevate an argument, defuse a loaded situation, or connect with a boss, colleague, or client.

••

FIVE SURE-FIRE HUMOR FORMULAS

How many times have you said it: "I just can't remember the punchline?" Like most women, you probably leave the more formal laugh lines–jokes–to men. But listen to science fiction wizard Issac Asimov, who wants to talk you out of your corner: "Why *can't* women remember jokes? Have they poor memories? Nonsense! They remember the price of every garment they bought and where they bought it. They know where everything is in the kitchen, including the mustard jar that any husband will swear, after a thorough search, is nowhere in the house. They are just defaulting on their responsibilities and as long as they do, they encourage men to put their heads together."

If we can remember stock prices, budget figures, and tiny details about clients, patients, and students, surely we can "remember" jokes. Maybe it will help if we stop using the word *joke*, and talk about using "planned humor." Here's the drill: Try using the following five humor formulas to add lightness and maintain your perspective and professionalism. These formulas are not punchlines; they are designed to help you convey a sense of lightness about people and problems on the job.

FORMULA #1: TWO PLUS, ONE MINUS

Use this formula to defuse tension by stating two positive and one negative side of the situation.

Picture yourself running several hours behind on submittal of a revamped budget. You might call your supervisor and soothe her impatience by saying, "Terry, I've found some reasonable places to make deeper cuts. I think you'll agree with my suggestions, and I'll have it on your desk about 2 hours later than I promised."

> *Architect to client:* "Your family room will be elegant, comfortable, and about two thousand dollars more than the original estimate."

> *Sales rep to customer* (who is demanding an immediate delivery of back-order inventory): "We've got the colors you want, we've got the sizes you want; and it will take about seven days to get them to you."

PRACTICE

Think of some recent bad or disappointing news you had to convey to your boss, client, or co-worker (for example, being over budget, out of inventory, having a project canceled, losing a client). How could you have softened the message using the "two plus, one minus" formula?

FORMULA #2: "DOES THIS MEAN...?"

To reduce stress, try an exaggerated extension of a loaded situation. Imagine that you have received word from above that another budget ax is expected at month's end. You gather your staff together, tell them of the cutting edge, and then add, "This probably means that we won't be having the office Christmas dinner at the Four Seasons."

> *Accountant to client* (sitting in accountant's office, reeling from the news of $10,000 of unexpected taxes): "This probably means that you won't be going to Paris in July."

> *You to your supervisee* (after listening to his litany of complaints about a co-worker): "Does this mean you don't want to share office space with him?"

List some recent stressful conversations in the office. How might you have added levity with a "Does this mean..." question.

FORMULA #3:
"THIS REMINDS ME OF..."

You can manage a variety of people and pressures with a lighter hand by using a variation of a "Barbara Walters question." Put a problem in perspective by a comic comparison with a current event or popular product, or by using an amusing metaphor. Imagine that you have been paired on a project with a co-worker who has made it clear she'd prefer another partner. You might acknowledge the problem and lighten the process by saying, "If East and West Germany can reunite, I'll bet we can work together on this project."

> *Software programmer to executive* (explaining why it takes so long to create a new program): "It's kind of like digging a ditch with a spoon."

> *Nurse to a patient* (receiving a dose of calcium carbonate): "This tastes like lemonade and works like Drano."

PRACTICE

Watch the news tonight and ask yourself which world scenarios comically compare with a crisis in your office (for example, a congressional budget fight, a front-page divorce, a troubled political campaign, the behavior of a deposed dictator). Listen to advertising slogans. Which ones might afford comic relief? For example, what were today's "Maalox moments"?

FORMULA #4: "I HEARD IT AT THE MOVIES"

Borrow a line from popular movies to gain comic relief from a difficult situation. Imagine that you are in the awkward position of explaining the indifference of one of your best clients to your boss. You could introduce the subject by saying, "I'm concerned about Al Taylor. He's beginning to sound a little like Rhett Butler. Frankly, he doesn't seem to give a damn."

> *You* (during a difficult negotiation with a customer, borrowing Marlon Brando's line from *The Godfather*): "Now, I'm going to make you an offer you can't refuse."

> *You to a supervisee* (as you sit down to discuss problems between you): "As Bette Davis once said, 'Fasten your seat belts, it's going to be a bumpy ride.' "

PRACTICE

List some memorable movie lines. For example, from *Cool Hand Luke*: "What we have here is a failure to

••

communicate." From *Gone with the Wind*: "I'll think
about it tomorrow." From *Dirty Harry*: "Read my lips."
Which ones fit recent stressful situations on the job?

FORMULA #5: SCHEHERAZADE

The legendary *Tales of 1,001 Nights* are stories of a spell-
binder named Scheherazade who saved her lovely neck
by telling her toady prince beguiling tales–one every
night. You can plan to save the day by using lighthearted
stories instead of jokes. The advantage of using stories is
that the action is one step removed. When you invite a colleague or client to survey the situation in the analogy of a
story, you allow him or her enough room to change position, or to gain new insight about an old problem–without losing face or becoming defensive.

Start with written sources; for example, *The Little,
Brown Book of Anecdotes* (Clifton Fadiman, editor), or
2,500 Anecdotes for All Occasions (Edmund Fuller). Read
biographies with an eye for anecdotes. Politicians relish
anecdotes; listen to their speeches with a new ear. Show
business personalities do too, especially when they appear on national television. Don't rule out the stories told
by the older generations of your family.

| PRACTICE |

Here are four favorite stories. After you read each one, list
a situation at work or home where you might use the tale
to add a light touch.

- *Chicken and Pig*
  A chicken was chatting with a nearby pig:
  "What a contribution we have made–ham and
  eggs. We are on breakfast tables all over the

world." The pig replied: "That's easy for you to say. You just have to make a contribution. But with me, it's a total commitment!"
(*Hint: to talk about motivation with employees, to discuss the career path of an employee.*)

- *Wine and Water*
Every year, a small farm village had a harvest celebration. There never seemed to be enough wine to drink. So one year, the villagers decided that every Friday night each family would add a little wine to a large oak barrel in the village square. By the next harvest, they would have enough wine to celebrate.
  For several months, every family brought wine faithfully to the square. Then, one by one, each family began to water down the wine they added to the barrel. By the time the harvest arrived, the wine was watery–undrinkable!
(*Hint: to encourage more involvement in the office, classroom, hospital.*)

- *Jascha Heifetz*
A young musician rushed up to the famed violinist Heifetz after a concert and said, "Oh, Mr. Heifetz, I'd give my *life* to play the violin like you!" He smiled and answered, "But, my dear, I *did*."
(*Hint: to inspire the staff, or to soothe an impatient fast-tracker.*)

- *The Wisest Man*
A husband and wife took their problems to the wisest man in town. Standing before the man

and his young apprentice, the husband told his tale of woe. After listening, the wise man nodded his head and said, "You are right in these matters." Then, the wife told her side of the relationship. The wise man listened, thought for a moment, and said, "You are absolutely right."

The young apprentice couldn't contain his confusion. "But, sir, you just told the husband *he* was right and the wife that *she* was right. They can't both be right!" At this point, the wise man smiled and said, "You know, you're right." (*Hint: to de-escalate an argument at work or soften a stalemate in a meeting.*)

FAIL-PROOF HUMOR: WHAT TO SAY IF YOU BOMB

Don't be discouraged if your early attempts at humor don't bring down the house. Remember that the goal of your planned humor—whether an anecdote or a line leased from Marlon Brando—is to communicate a sense of lightness. With that goal, you can't fail as long as you convey that you have a sense of humor. Learn to settle for evoking a smile or watching a furrowed brow soften.

What if you attempt a "big" joke and bomb?

Yvonne G. was in the middle of telling a joke at a national nursing conference. Suddenly she faltered and said, "Oh, no! I've forgotten the punchline." But she quickly recovered by using a line she had heard elsewhere: "The brain is a marvelous thing, isn't it? It starts working the moment you get out of bed and it doesn't stop working until you stand up in front of an audience!" The audience laughed and applauded.

Practice adapting Yvonne's line to potential stressful moments in your work life: "The brain is a wonderful thing; it doesn't stop working until you (pick up an actuarial chart, sit down at the computer, try to cut the budget, etc.)." Or be prepared with other recovery lines you can use, borrowed from experts like Johnny Carson:

> "I guess you had to be there to appreciate it."

> "Just raise your hand if I say something funny."

> "I'll have to fire my writers, after that one."

Beware of using humorous styles that are guaranteed to fail.

FAIL-SURE HUMOR: THREE MIRTHFUL MANEUVERS THAT ARE GUARANTEED TO FAIL

AVOID PLAYING THE COURT JESTER

Keep in mind that the court jester, after all, is a fool. Your use of humor, particularly in the office, should be frequent but not constant. Sandra B., 42, a county administrator and nonstop wit, was referred to by a male executive as "our little entertainer." Said Sandra, "I had to learn to use humor more sparingly, so that other people would realize it was a skill."

Fran G., 27, a top sales rep for a line of bakery products, dressed up as a turkey one Thanksgiving week to convince a customer to increase his order of poultry stuffing. Recalls Fran, "Not only didn't he increase his order, but he was really insulted; he thought I was calling *him* a turkey!"

As Sandra and Fran learned, the most effective mirth at work is both understated and occasional. So save the stand-up routine for open-mike at the comedy club, and the costumes for Halloween.

DON'T MAKE YOURSELF
THE BUTT OF THE JOKE

Sharon G., 42, a superbly talented educator, closed a recent meeting with some "planned humor" that made me squirm. "My doctor recently told me that I was too fat," she said. "I said to him, 'I want a second opinion.' So he said, 'Well, you're also ugly.'" Yes, everyone in the meeting laughed, but at her expense.

Keep a check on self-deprecating humor at work. Careless cracks about yourself will weaken your professional credibility and undermine your confidence. What may work for Joan Rivers or Phyllis Diller in Vegas spells disaster in the office for you.

Beverly O., 42, a public relations consultant, draws a fine line: "I enjoy self-deprecating humor that comes up because I'm feeling good about myself–then I don't mind joking about the situation. I try to avoid the kind of humor where I'm saying it first so that you won't say it."

REFUSE TO MUD WRESTLE

Off-color jokes are off-limits for working women. "I have an uncanny ability to remember jokes," explains

Vivian B., 46, a bank officer. "I got in the habit of telling dicey jokes to a supervisor a couple of notches up. Then he began to seek *me* out to tell me filthy jokes, racist and sexist—not funny, either. I guess I gave him the wrong message; he thought that because I told off-color stories, I must be a trash bin."

Reserve the gamey stories for friends and lovers who know what an elegant woman you are.

*I*NCREASING THE *O*DDS

Did you hear the one about the woman who desperately wanted to win the lottery? Every Saturday morning for six months before the drawings, she would pray: "Oh, God, please let me win the lottery." One Saturday morning as she prayed, she heard the melodious voice of God: "Joan, will you do me a favor?" She stammered, "Anything, God, of course." Said God, "Would you meet me halfway: would you please *buy a ticket*?"

The reward of using humor formulas requires that you take a chance. Now you are ready to officially put mirth to work.

PART THREE

···

FUNNY
BUSINESS

CHAPTER SIX

....

GRACE
UNDER PRESSURE

Sally N., 46, sailed through her meeting with the CEO, the last of four grueling interviews for an executive vice-president's job in a prestigious development firm. The interview ended, she moved toward the door, and her navy-blue, wrap-around skirt dropped to her ankles. Clad below the waist in only a slip, she picked up the skirt, linked her arm in the CEO's, and walked down the hall to the restroom. When she returned, re-skirted, he offered her the job.

Most of us cannot imagine how Sally showed such grace under pressure, yet we do understand the cost of being too serious in awkward or uncertain moments. Explains Melissa C., 34, a small-business owner, "When I'm negotiating with a new client, I'm so afraid of making a mistake and I get so tense, I can feel a rash crawl up my neckline. But if I don't relax, I can't pick up on the essential signals from the client; I miss the give-and-take that is so important in negotiation."

This chapter offers examples and exercises to explain how lightening up can help you maintain your composure and establish a strong presence even when the heat is on.

Surviving the Comedy of Your Errors

Studies have shown that up to 80 percent of us feel like impostors at one time or another, and mistakes and missteps make us feel all the more exposed. Like Peggy and Keri, you may find the roots of these feelings growing under your feet.

Peggy H., 33, an accountant, explains her fear of trying: "My desire to be perfect limited my participation; if I didn't say anything, I couldn't be criticized. I was able to trace this feeling back to my relationship with my father—the anger he showed when he corrected me, I felt that if I didn't give the right answer, he would love me less. I realized I was carrying those feelings into work."

Keri S., 30, a broker, talks about the lighter side: "My humor is a kind of honesty. As a kid I was always apologizing, always being overly honest. Now when I make an error, humor is an honest way to acknowledge it. Usually with a mistake, the other person is uncomfortable, too. My lightness puts them at ease; they can laugh, too."

The key to surviving the comedy of your errors is to make fun of the situation and not yourself. A fine example is my friend Hallie, a psychologist who has a wonderful, light sense of herself. Several years ago, she stepped up to the podium to address an international conference in

Germany. Before she opened her mouth, a screen behind her fell forward and landed squarely on her toe. The audience gasped, and Hallie leaned into the microphone to say, "I'd like to begin my keynote address with an important question: *Is there a doctor in the house?*"

As a good-humor woman, you can learn to shine brightly with your own unique sense of style. Bonnie M., 35, is the owner of a large printing company. When an irate customer calls with a complaint about a misprint in the proofs, she adds the grace note of humor. "I always include a zany alternative as one of the client's options—I might say, 'You have two choices: we can strip and change the typeface by hand, or we can leave it and see how many people notice.' "

PLANNING TO *BE IMPERFECT*

Managing awkward moments and mishaps can sometimes be a matter of planning, since many jobs have predictable problems that call for a light-handed response. For many of you, your job involves presentations—to clients, customers, trainees. As a savvy speaker, you can be prepared for potential problems on the podium. Here's a sampling of planned humor from author and humor consultant Michael Iapoce:

> When the lights go out: *"This is taking energy conservation too far."*

> When a microphone feeds back or squeals: *"Don't be alarmed; this is only a test."*

> When a slide projector jams: *"This is what happens when you buy your slide carousel at K-Mart."*

··

> When a loud crash is heard during the
> presentation: *"This includes the musical portion
> of my program."*
>
> When there is silence at the beginning of a
> question-and-answer session: *"Did E. F. Hutton
> just speak?"*

Picture yourself at the end of your presentation in a strategic planning session. As usual, one of your team members asks a long, rambling "question" that is really a push, designed to throw you off-balance. How can you redirect her hostility—without showing yours?

> *DO YOU:*
>
> **A.** Plant your feet firmly and give her an equally
> long, factual response?
>
> **B.** Sarcastically say: "Thank you for your
> feedback."
>
> **C.** Ask her: "Can you repeat the question?"

A. is all too serious and *defensive*. B. is an *aggressive* response that will add to her animosity. You'll be safe with C.: a *mirthful* response, making fun of the situation (she is pretending to ask a question) that allows you to demonstrate composure and your control of the moment.

The ability to anticipate awkward moments exists in every working relationship. For example, Teresa R., 32, a stockbroker, explains, "Very early in my relationship with a client, I talk to him or her about what to expect—how I research an opportunity, how I make recommendations. Then I always add, 'and believe it or not, I'm not always right.'" I find clients really relate to my honesty and usually they laugh and say something like: 'I understand; just keep me posted.'" In Teresa's acknowledgment of an imperfect future, she glows with the credibility and confidence that is the essence of lightening up.

PRACTICE

List two situations on your job that predictably lead to awkward moments or opportunities for error. What kind of comic relief can you plan to use next time?

THE ART OF BEING AT EASE

When the members of Nebraska's state legislature returned for a recent session, they were greeted by Governor Kay Orr handing out bouquets of flowers. Governor Orr fondly remembers the comment of one legislator: "Maybe she is confident enough to still be feminine."

Oh, that word "feminine." Are you ready for a lighter look? We listened for years to the crippling advice that the key to the "Old Boy's Club" was to deny our special "feminine" traits. (See Chapter 2, Mistaken Belief #3.) And wouldn't you know it, our symbolic hiding was accomplished in the guise of fashion. In this case, style was really an issue of substance.

Said Peggy Noonan, Reagan speechwriter and author of the best-selling *What I Saw at the Revolution*, "I think our first impulse going out into the world of business and politics was to use clothes as kind of protective coloration; to blend in with the blue pinstripes. But we're not self-conscious and vulnerable anymore. We have arrived; we are here, and we can be ourselves." Gloria Steinem, editor of *Ms.*, agrees: "Fashion in the present means being an individual and finding oneself."

This discovery and comfortable expression of yourself is your highest achievement as a good-humor woman. It is not a question of costume—or of jumping on top of your desk, singing, "I gotta be me," dressed in a leather micro-mini—but one of allowing your unique personality to create a powerful presence on the job. When your oh-so-serious intention denies your special qualities, you lose an opportunity to build long-term working alliances with clients, co-workers, and bosses. "People like to work with someone from a place of pleasure," explains one successful real estate developer, "and I can't build that kind of connection by being all business. I need to share my sense of humor and my own perspectives with clients."

We can learn from Mary Ann J., 32, as she describes her growing comfort and credibility as a financial advisor.

> I used to be apologetic and uncomfortable about my vacations; I worried that clients would think I wasn't serious, that I wasn't in the office every day, monitoring their investments. But when I reviewed my track record with clients, I realized that most of my continuing business came from connecting with people—not from cold calls or pursuing prospects. I have learned to relax and be more spontaneous. When I let people know about me—whether it is my scuba diving vacation, my own investments, or my time in the Peace Corps—I can build deeper, more trusting relationships. Clients now send their kids and friends to me. I am relaxed enough to tell them, "I want to be your family doctor of finance."

LAUGHING WITH DIFFICULT PEOPLE

Humor is a graceful means of managing tough customers, bosses, and co-workers without aging in dog years. Your lighter touch can help you connect with even the most frustrating folks. The key to defusing the tension is inviting the other person to consider the humor in the situation.

With her fussiest client, one personnel manager introduces a new job candidate by telephoning to say, "I know we both have such discriminating tastes and that no one will be good enough for this position, but I'm sending someone to meet you tomorrow anyway." Tina R., 45, a public relations manager, lengthens the fuse of a workaholic client by means of a standing joke. She walks into her monthly meetings with him and comments, "The only reason I came to this meeting so early is because you always have such good donuts." He always replies, "There are no donuts; I've been working all night–I ate them."

Your good humor can be the softest yet most effective form of persuasion. Explains social worker Pat S., 38, "Whenever the agency director and I are on the opposite sides of a problem, I slip in a non-argument. I might say, 'If we do what I suggest, the world will probably come to an end,' and he jumps in, laughing, 'Not the entire world, but a significant portion.' This lightness keeps him flexible; buys me time before his resistance is set in concrete."

Savor the success of Shari R., 25, a sales manager, who became a shameless punster with an indecisive purchasing executive of software. She knew about his farm in Connecticut; so she bought a basketful of plastic farm tools at Woolworth's and attached a pun to each one (for example, a tractor with the message, "This is to plow the other proposals from your desk"). She called to ask for five minutes of his time, with the promise: "You will make your decision on the spot." When she delivered the toys, he read the messages, laughed appreciatively, and said, "You're right; this has gone on for too long." He picked up the phone and authorized the sale.

USING THE *MBA* FORMULA

To polish your response to people pressures on the job, try this three-step "MBA formula"—a formula few of us learned in business school.

STEP 1: MIRROR

Make fun of your shared situation by "mirroring" the situation or playing with the image at hand. For example, when Deborah Norville replaced the popular Jane Pauley as co-anchor on NBC's "Today Show," NBC staffers dubbed her "the stewardess," because of her perky manner. Norville responded to the unflattering nickname by dressing the part at a writers' meeting. She playfully mirrored their insult—and gained their goodwill—by wearing a blue jacket, blue pants, white shirt, and a wings pin, serving them coffee from a beverage cart.

PRACTICE

Imagine that an angry customer is shouting into the telephone: "You say your company has one hundred years of experience! So why can't you get my bill straight?" How can you manage her anger—and gain her trust?

Hint: Try mirroring her image. You might say, "Yes, we are one hundred years old, and from the look of your bill, you must think we're getting senile."

STEP 2: BORROW

Create comic relief with a comic comparison ("this reminds me of") or a borrowed line. The last few presidential campaigners have found their strongest voices by borrowing from popular culture; long before cheesecake ruined his career, Gary Hart was skewered by a line Walter Mondale borrowed from a burger ad. Republicans Reagan and Bush have borrowed a succession of Clint Eastwood-isms.

PRACTICE

What can you say to the promising but exasperating new staff member who has mistakenly shredded an important file?

Hint: Try to turn the tension around with a line from a familiar ad, saying, "This gives a whole new meaning to that Alka-Seltzer commercial where the guy says, 'I can't believe I ate the whole thing.' "

What other lines can you borrow?

STEP 3: ANTICIPATE

Use humor to anticipate resistance or defensiveness from co-workers or clients. Put their words in your mouth, asking, for example: "Have you had your aggravation for the day?" or "Just when you had your whole day planned out, I call for an emergency meeting."

PRACTICE

A colleague has failed to meet a project deadline. How can you get Johnny-Come-Lately to respond in a more timely manner?

Hint: Say what you imagine he's thinking. For example, "I'm just calling to nag you about turning in your numbers for the McKinsey project."

What other openers will work for you?

The easiest route to anticipation is to offer an irresistible invitation to laughter. When calling a boss, client, or colleague with questionable news, simply say, "You'll really appreciate this because I know you have a great sense of humor."

SILENT COMEDY REVISITED

Remember that you can easily look on the lighter side of people and professional pratfalls without saying a word. Take, for example, Hilary R., 33, a Washington state governor's aide, who relies on the kind of silent comedy we played with in Chapter 4. "When Governor Gardner was inaugurated, he gave a wonderful speech about risk-taking and stated, 'Out of every ten decisions I make, four are a mistake.' Now, whenever *I* make a mistake, I picture myself saying to him, 'Governor, this is one of my *four*.' "

Much of your capacity to see the "funny business" in the serious agenda of your career lies in your willingness to relabel stressful situations in comic terms and remain confident, flexible, and approachable. I have asked hundreds of working women and men to share the images that add grace notes to on-the-job pressure. Here are some of their lighter asides.

When I fall behind, I picture myself pedaling a bicycle without a chain.

When I have to redo a proposal, I picture myself in *The Perils of Pauline*; I'm tied to a railroad track and a train is coming.

Whenever I make a mistake, I remind myself that this piece of business is only one tiny part of the total scheme of my life, which includes friends and politics and music.

When my boss is particularly stubborn, I picture him as Archie Bunker in his armchair—I know he is not going to change.

Last year when I traveled to China, I realized that there are millions of people who don't care about what happens in my office!

I recall the exact moment when I discovered the role of silent comedy in achieving a state of professional grace. I was teaching a management seminar to a group of bankers in Minnesota. Unfortunately, my seminar was preceded by an elaborate dinner—open bar, wine with dinner, cognac with coffee; I had never seen such a relaxed group of financiers. Very early in the seminar, I found my attention drawn to three gentlemen in the front row who laughed uproariously any time I said something remotely funny. They were beginning to distract the rest of the group.

I could feel my thermostat climb and my concentration fragment; I was on the verge of sarcastic comment, when suddenly I had the silliest image. I played with the image and I felt my shoulders relax, my focus and my confidence return as I pictured myself saying to them—in my best fifth-grade teacher's voice—"Would you like to share that with the rest of us?"

The image was so compelling and amusing that I went the next step and told the group. Addressing myself to the gabbing gentlemen, I said, "I am watching you enjoy this seminar and chat among yourselves and I realize what all of the fifth-grade teachers of the world felt like when they asked if we wanted to share with the rest of the class." The three men laughed, stopped talking, and listened attentively for the rest of the evening.

CHAPTER SEVEN

LAUGHTER IS
THE BEST MANAGEMENT

*M*arla W., 29, was delighted to learn of her promotion to first-line supervisor in a high-tech company. She immediately understood her biggest challenge: "Today I was drinking coffee with the gang, complaining about the boss; tomorrow, I am going to *be* the boss. How can I establish my authority?" As the group assembled for their first team meeting, Marla began by saying, "I know things seem different around here; but I don't want you to think of me as your boss, I want you to continue to think of me as your friend. You know, the kind of friend who is *always right!*" The group laughed with approval, and Marla took the first step in establishing her authority as a new manager.

Marla's job, like that of all managers, will be to get her job done through the supervision of other people. In this chapter, you'll meet good-humored managers who enlist humor as a means of educating, motivating, or reducing staff stress and who rave about the power of laughter. Says one savvy manager, "Without humor, I get exactly what I ask for. With humor, I get so many delightful surprises."

SIX WAYS TO USE LAUGHTER AS A MANAGEMENT TOOL

In doing the background research to conduct my corporate seminars, I find that a company's sense of humor is the clearest gauge of the corporate climate. For example, account managers at Ketchum Advertising send one another Gary Larson's *The Far Side* sketches; managers at Du Pont post cartoons about time crunches; and Kodak managers share jokes lampooning customers' behavior. One CEO offered a dollar-per-month award for the best cartoon about what was going on in the company—a practice he described as "the best money I ever spent on research; I learned more about the pressures and concerns of my group than from any survey."

More and more companies are realizing the rich opportunity of laughing at themselves. At a GTE executive retreat, a puppet named Gertie Glitch engages in cheeky repartee with an executive VP; at a Nordstrom annual employee meeting, managers sing a parody of Michael Jackson's "Beat It," called "Charge It"; attendees at New York Life's Executive Officers Weekend watched two top executives (in various costume changes) enact 100 years of the insurance company's history.

Being the boss is no joke, but as a manager, here are six ways you can use humor as a management tool.

TO DELIVER BAD NEWS

Hearing bad news, most employees experience a combination of angry, anxious, and defensive feelings. Research indicates that these emotions prevent them from taking in further information or engaging in the kind of problem-solving a crisis may require. Listen, then, to the manager who has developed a ritual of singing bad news in mock-operatic style. "The computers are down," he sings. "When will they be back on line?" choruses his laughing staff. Admire the wit of a San Francisco PR manager of a paper company, who received some devastating press about the release of dioxins from one of the company's paper mills. He addressed a problem-solving session with his staff with this opener: "The good news is that the name of our company is on everyone's lips—the bad news is that the lips are curled."

How can you laugh, when you know I'm down? Because, explains Professor David Abramis of California State University at Long Beach, laughter releases the tension that keeps people from focusing on their work.

Imagine that you just received word from senior management that your department's program budget has been cut 25 percent. In today's meeting, you must announce it to your staff; how can you keep them from killing the messenger?

DO YOU SAY:

A. *"I've got some bad news; senior management has fallen out of love with our programs."*

B. *"The good news is, you get to keep your jobs. The bad news is, our budget has been cut by 25 percent."*

C. *"When I got word of our program budget for next year, I had a very 'zen' experience: I found myself contemplating nothingness!"*

Avoid A.; making senior management a scapegoat won't help rally your troops. B. is bad news, too; raising the uncertainty of job loss along with funding cuts is guaranteed to elevate blood pressures. Stick with C.; making fun of the situation will help create the esprit de corps you will need to do more work with less funding.

To Change Behavior

Formal appraisal systems exist in most job settings, but informal humor can be the fastest route to changing the staff behavior that makes you want to consider a career change. Take the example of the manager who received an appallingly bad report from a new employee. She listed her criticisms and attached a Band-Aid to the list, saying, "Can this be fixed?"

Humor educator Esther Blumenthal tells the story of the Atlanta manager, tired of all the whining in her department, who posted a sign on an empty jar above the coffee machine, suggesting: "Whisper your complaints in here and put a lid on it." Another manager, building on this theme, silenced the moaners by announcing a "weekly whine-in" at 3 P.M. Thursdays, with complaining forbidden at all other times. Attendance dropped to zero after three weeks.

Another smart manager, perplexed by the long lines in the neighborhood branch bank she supervised, discovered that the lines grew because tellers tried to postpone dealing with well-known "tough customers." Her solution: offering a "Customer Story of the Month Award," based on the most outrageous encounter with a demanding customer. The long lines vanished within a week.

Match your wits with the managers of a southern aerospace company faced with employees who had grown lazy about following plant safety practices. Which approach would you recommend to them?

SHOULD THEY:

A. *Plan an all-day safety conference, complete with alarming safety statistics and a film showing tragic outcomes of carelessness.*

B. *Institute a system of fines and disciplinary action for infractions of safety rules.*

C. *Create a cartoon campaign featuring characters who refused to play it safe (for example, The Old Timer: "I been here for twenty years; you don't have to tell me the rules." The Macho Man/Woman: "I don't need to follow the exact rules; I'm careful.")*

Both A. and B. had been tried, in fact, and failed. The company found C. to be a surprising success. When employees had the opportunity to look at their own attitudes about safety in a comic light, their defensiveness about noncompliance was reduced and they were willing to reconsider their attitudes and actions.

TO CONFRONT DIFFICULT ISSUES

Humor softens the edge of confrontive issues, allowing you to approach staffers and dismantle brick walls. One human-resources executive returned after a two-week vacation to find that a number of important decisions had been made by a single staff member. She confronted the staffer by asking, "I've been watching the Iran-Contra hearings on my vacation and what I want to know is, what don't I know and when didn't I know it?"

Or consider the example of the manager who raised the issue of personal calls during business hours by playing on an old phone company advertising campaign. His announcement to his assembled staff: "We want you to reach out and touch someone, but not on company time."

Remember that sometimes *your* behavior is the thorny issue. One light-handed supervisor walked into an angry staff meeting with a bull's-eye pinned to his chest. The group shouted with laughter and moved quickly to discuss their grievances.

Picture yourself as a sales manager whose department's performance the previous month has been extremely flat. The best means of motivating them is to avoid attacking the group—they are already aware of their failure. Instead of saying, "From the size of these sales figures, it looks like some of you have been taking vacation time," you might try a lighter line, one that makes fun of the situation: "The last time an order went out of this office was two weeks ago—and that was for two coffees and a cinnamon roll."

TO BUILD A SENSE OF TEAM

The teams that work best together are the ones that have the most inside jokes. The definition of an inside joke is one whose humor is seldom understood by outsiders. Have you ever tried to retell outside of work something funny that happened in the office? You are laughing hysterically while your friend's eyes start to glaze over in boredom. Still, the power of inside humor to unite a workforce as a team is this clubbish/members-only quality. As a manager, you'll be wise to use humor as a team-building technique. It will allow your work group to identify with one another and to support one another despite shared pressure.

I applaud the mirthful manager who equipped all of his employees in the data processing shop with green tinted 3-D glasses. Whenever the computer systems were down and co-workers rushed in to complain, they would find the staff dressed for another dimension! I love to picture the real estate development firm with a three-foot gong in the office reception area. Whenever anyone signed a deal, they would ring the gong and all agents would rush out of their individual offices and cheer.

Whenever I consult with a newly merged company, I encourage the new work teams to develop inside jokes. When US West Communications was formed, the merger involved employees from three quite different cities: Seattle, Omaha, and Denver. The humor at the time of the merger was, to put it mildly, adversarial. For example: *Q:* I need to go to Omaha for a meeting; do I need shots? *A:* Yes, if you are staying for more than a night. At a three-city managerial retreat, I asked them to create a bumper sticker that would incorporate aspects of all three cities. Their inside joke: "I brake for rattlesnakes, cows, and slugs."

PRACTICE

List the possibilities for creating inside jokes for your work team. Possible sources of humor include local geography, the competition, infamous customers, cafeteria food, telephone tag, parking spaces, paperwork, length of meetings, deadlines, computer snafus, and other shared pressure points.

To Manage Change

Help your staff manage rapid change by allowing them to laugh all the way. For example, when ARCO Chemical was in the process of a major restructuring, a memo surfaced announcing: "The initials for ARCO now stand for 'Aimlessly Reorganizing Corporate Organization.'" In Washington state, when Old National Bank and People's Bank were in the process of merging, both companies' employees referred to themselves as "The Old People's Bank."

A financial services company spent several hundred thousand dollars on an unpopular new customer training program. When employees resisted and failed to master new techniques, the top management decided to sweeten the skills with laughter: they sponsored a "Customer Mistakes Olympics." In order to win, each player had to know the new skills so they could reverse them. The program was a hilarious success.

When the humor-amid-chaos is initiated by you, you can communicate a sense of emotional support and the confidence that the change can be managed. I'm tickled by the manager at Tektronix whose department was responsible for implementing a new, unpopular policy: She gave each person a desk nameplate with his or her first name and the last name Dangerfield. As she explained, "You won't get no respect for a long time around here."

PRACTICE

What kinds of changes are occurring in your workplace? How might you use humor to help employees manage the stress of change?

To Communicate Solidarity

Use your sense of humor to convey your connection with employee concerns. A smiling nod or a sympathetic chuckle when listening to an employee's horror story will strengthen your alliance. Maybe you'd like to go further, like the group of executives at Ohio Bell who dressed up like the California Raisins to join in the employees' campaign for United Way, or the CEO who made an unexpected visit and found one department celebrating a successful project by wearing outrageous hats. He returned to his office, grabbed a pair of Mickey Mouse ears his grandson had given him, and rejoined the celebration as a Mouseketeer.

Imagine the ways you might strengthen your working alliance with staff members. As a manager, you will be most successful if you convey your sense of solidarity with your unique style. Which one of these scenarios sounds most like you?

A. The manager who closed a heated staff meeting vote with the comment, "Well, *that* was easy, wasn't it?"

B. The manager who motivated her staff by borrowing a line from a Nike ad campaign. She had T-shirts made with the line "JUST DO IT."

C. The manager who opened every weekly meeting with five minutes of "Believe It or Not" stories–with employees sharing their most maddening, funny encounters with customers.

THE OFFICE THAT PLAYS TOGETHER: TEN TECHNIQUES FOR INCREASING CREATIVITY THROUGH LEVITY

Do you remember the classic "Motown" scene on "L.A. Law" a few seasons ago? Two young associates were working late, growing short on energy and shorter on ideas. As they rested their heads on the table, one suggested that they take a dance break. Soon the sound of Marvin Gaye's "I Heard It Through the Grapevine" filled the room and they were laughing, whirling, jumping to dance on the conference table—until they were startled by the unexpected entrance of one of the senior partners. Embarrassed, but energized, they were able to work creatively for several hours longer.

Laughter and lightness are often the path to tension reduction and creative problem resolution. Creativity, after all, involves switching into a mood where new ideas can be generated. There is mounting clinical evidence to prove the maxim of Kodak founder Max Eastman: "Laughter puts your brain, your central nervous system and your whole being into a state of free play."

Why is playing an essential job skill? A fascinating study, completed at the University of California at Berkeley in the 1970s, explored the styles of faculty members labeled as "most creative" by their colleagues. Test results indicated not higher IQ scores, but that these professors took longer to study problems—played with them more. The difference was, these highly creative people knew how to switch themselves into a "playful mood," something the study describes as being more "childlike." Don't forget how many companies began with someone tinkering in a garage.

Other recent studies by Israeli psychologist Avner Ziv indicate that participation in a humorous experience before a brainstorming session encourages divergent, creative thinking. Cox Communications Company has taken this message literally and bars coats and ties from creativity sessions. Instead, they offer a rack of 15 loud Hawaiian print shirts. The president notes, "Everyone laughs and grumbles, but by the time they change shirts, they are relaxed and ready to begin problem-solving."

Try a kaleidoscope of ideas to manage meetings to increase the sense of spontaneity, creativity, and play.

- *Begin the meeting by listening to a comedy soundtrack or watching a short comic film or video.* "Monty Python's" John Cleese created a number of punchy videos for his Chicago-based company, Video Arts.

- *Make a videotape of the problem at hand.* One company's collection department created a now classic re-dub of the hapless "Saturday Night Live" cartoon character Mr. Bill, called Mr. Bill Collector (Oh nooooooh!).

- *Appoint a cartoonist.* At Indiana University, the house attorney is an amateur cartoonist. His assignment at the board meetings is to create comic sketch versions of thorny problems. At critical moments, these drawings circulate among the board of trustees to dissolve tension and facilitate problem-solving.

- *Anoint a fool.* This is a favorite of creativity consultant Roger Oech, who reminds us that in the Middle Ages the kings and queens had jesters to protect them from sycophants and self-motivated advisors and to provide a fresh– if absurd–perspective. Take turns being assigned to act as "the fool" or the "humor captain" who brings cartoons or designs a playful activity for break time.

- *Represent the problem or goal visually.* Offer crayons, watercolors, clay, straws, and stick-pins to create a portrait of an issue or direction being discussed.

- *Create a metaphor or a comic comparison for the problem or direction of the agenda.* Pose the questions: What animal or color does this client or project remind you of? What soup or novel does the project budget resemble?

- *Put on blindfolds.* Just listen to the flow of conversation and ideas; have all participants accentuate their sense of hearing.

- *Bring other senses into play.* Pass materials with various textures around the conference table— for example, sandpaper, burlap, silk, velvet. Think about which materials resemble the problem or the solution you seek.

- *Roast the client.* One PR firm, when frustrated with the many demands of a client, releases tension and generates new plans by taking part of a meeting to do a Don Rickles–style "roast" of the client and the product.

- *Bring out the worst.* When I consult with advertising firms that have reached a creative block on a particular campaign, I invite them to shift gears and consider the *worst* possible campaign, highlighting the unattractive aspects of the client's product or service. Said one advertising executive, "Our best ideas come when we are playing hard."

· ·

| **PRACTICE** |

Imagine that you are appointed "humor captain" of your next staff meeting. Which of the playful paths to creativity appeal to you? Which ones would fit best with your management style and the culture of your workplace?

Remember, too, that lightening up in the hours after work is just as important as bringing a sense of play into the workplace. Don't get caught in the trap of handing out your business cards at your nephew's wedding. Plan to encourage your staff to renew themselves after work. As one CEO told me, "I want my employees to relax after hours because leisure and play are the source of creativity."

Follow this advice and go to the movies, enroll in a Thai cooking class, take up scuba diving, learn magic tricks, explore your local science museum, browse in bookstores, plan a vacation in Barcelona. Above all, learn to pause and enjoy life after work. Slow down so that your good humor and creativity as a manager can catch up with you.

PART FOUR

CAUTION:
MEN AT WORK

*C*HAPTER *E*IGHT

••

HUMOR:
HIS AND HERS

*K*aren M., 38, an insurance agent, remembers every morsel of a dessert she ordered eight years ago at a dinner with a dozen men from her department. After the entrees were cleared, the waiter appeared with a lavish pastry cart. Karen's boss asked the waiter to describe each dessert in detail and turned to her and asked, "What will *you* have, Karen?" He smiled as she ordered the mocha almond torte. Then, one by one, each of the twelve men declined dessert.

"I turned bright crimson," recalls Karen. "I wanted to grab the waiter by the coattails and change my order. When the torte was set before me, I wanted to crawl under the table. There I was, a beginner in the company–the perfect target for a set-up."

As a new recruit, Karen was unprepared for this ambush, but it was the kind of humor her male colleagues learned to enjoy at an early age. In this chapter, we will explore the difference between men's and women's humor, offering techniques for confronting and controlling men's often aggressive style of joking–without imitating it.

VIVE LA DIFFÉRENCE

Fascinating studies by psychologist Paul McGhee demonstrate that in the nursery school years there appear to be few differences in how much boys and girls laugh, attempt to be funny, or enjoy hostile humor. Yet by middle childhood (ages 6–11) boys score higher than girls in all aspects of humor—more laughter, more clowning, more hostility expressed in humor.

You don't have to eavesdrop on the jungle gym to discover that little girls hate being the target of jokes—and that little boys seem to relish it. We all remember the sting, the quick tears that wouldn't stop even if a boy said he was "only teasing." Somehow teasing meant something different to us than to our boyish tormentors; at best, we responded with a sickly grin, more often we were silenced, tearful. Not only could sticks and stones break our bones, as the ditty went, but names could always hurt us. We just didn't get in on the joke.

Years later, women are greeted at work and in love by a variety of male joking behaviors including practical jokes, puns, and—still the most bewildering—bantering or "ranking" with another person as the target. "I've heard men say the most bone-crushing things to each other and then laugh and go out to lunch together," says one bank manager. "If someone said those things to me, I'd need the afternoon off to recover!"

Women at work express amazement at the subjects men "rank" or tease each other about: hairlines and waistlines, athletic performance, sexual skills, sales figures, tax problems, financial blunders. "Most male humor," observes an accountant, "seems to improve the atmosphere at someone else's expense."

Case in point: David H., a prominent architect, arrived at a design commission meeting wearing a richly textured sports jacket, yellow tie, and matching yellow pocket handkerchief. "That's quite an outfit, David," said one man. "How'd you tie the tie so it came out of your pocket?" asked another. "He must have learned that working in a restaurant, folding napkins," commented a third.

How is women's humor different from men's? The short answer is that men's humor can be like a Hollywood Friars Club roast—all playful insults and mock-hostile slapstick; while women's humor is like an episode of TV's "Designing Women"—empathic and consoling, making a small comedy out of shared experiences. Here's how three good-humored women define the difference.

> Women's humor is right brain: intuitive, metaphoric, empathic—stressful situations remind us of funny ones; men's humor is left brain: rational and literal—an aggressive arrow aimed for the target.

> When we slip on a banana peel, we laugh at how absurd we look; when a man slips, we worry if he's hurt. When we see another woman slip, we feel empathy; we know how we'd feel in her situation. When a man sees another man slip on a banana peel, he just laughs and enjoys it.

> Men see humor as open season; women respect certain personal taboos. I can't imagine a woman saying to another woman: "Looks like you'll have to move your belt over a couple of notches."

Another essential difference between men's humor and women's may be in the ways that men and women

....

label the experience of being the target of a joke or insult.
For a woman, casual insults about her work habits or personal life are often taken literally and experienced as offensive and painful–as if they were an accurate description of herself. "When women get teased," says Monica M.,
32, a real estate broker, "we get angry or hurt and this
gives men even more ammunition and power." They can
say, 'You're fun when you're mad.'"

For men, the enjoyment of the snide aside resembles
what anthropologist A. R. Radcliffe-Brown calls a "joking relationship" with equal parts friendliness and hostility. In this kind of relationship, teasing and insults are
tolerated with the understanding that no one takes of-
fense. Unlike women, men seem to understand that underneath the hostile banter is an important message:
"This is play."

When we observe men at work and in their personal
lives, we see them using humor as communication used to
express and decompress feelings of anger, competition,
and even affection. One man took his closest male friend
to dinner on his birthday and gave him a lavish book with
a card inscribed: "Happy Birthday. You are a real jerk."

Joseph Heller, whose novel *Catch-22* captured the essence of male companionship, has been quoted suggesting that male humor is an indirect form of empathy. "Men
find it easier to be cruel than to commiserate. For both the
man making the remark and the man who is the object of
it–by making wisecracks we are really expressing empathy and compassion in our fashion. As if to say, 'We understand each other. I understand that I could be–and have
been–as vulnerable as you.'"

Since it seems unlikely that the Equal Employment
Opportunity Commission will be able to enforce victim-
less humor in the workplace, male bantering can be

expected to dominate. As you succeed, you will become a more frequent witness to men's raucous ranking and—increasingly—be the target of it. As a good-humor woman at work, you can learn to change the way you react when the joke is on you.

WHAT TO DO WHEN THE JOKE'S ON YOU

"When I was growing up, I was taught to be a little magnolia blossom, to get what I wanted by flirting," laments Tanya S., a city official. "My brother and my father used to tease me and I'd cry and cry, until the day I learned to tease them back. Then *I* learned the power of humor." Says another little sister who learned to play, "To this day, all I have to say to my brother David (now 40) is 'Poor Footchie' and he will fly into a rage."

I promised not to suggest that you imitate male humor, but rather that you figure out a way to get in on the joke. Once again, the key will be in making fun of the situation. For example, when Karen M. looks back on her ill-fated mocha torte, she says, "If those guys set me up today, I'd handle it with humor. When my dessert arrived, I would slowly savor each mouthful and exclaim about what they were missing. I might even call the waiter and ask for twelve forks so they could all taste."

As women succeed in jobs of every description, they discover the power of humor to maintain perspective and control. Joanna B., 41, a public utilities manager, explains, "When dealing with office humor, my power position depends on my reaction, my ability to give and take. If I can say or do something quickly, they leave me alone; if I show them that I am uncomfortable, they have a field day."

So imagine this: You return to work after a fifty-dollar haircut. You are feeling well-coiffed and confident until several of your male co-workers start to comment: "Boy, is it short!" and "Sure makes the gray show." Once you rule out attacking them with your desk scissors, what are your choices?

DO YOU SAY:

A. "At least I've got some hair to turn gray."

B. (Hands smoothing hair) "Do you really think so?"

C. "I figure our clients will find me distinguished."

Let's immediately rule out A. as too *aggressive*. Learning to field insults from men is not the occasion for your enrollment in the Don Rickles School of Broadcasting. As much as we would like to believe otherwise, men who insult each other can punch dangerously close to home and still be perceived as witty and amusing, but a woman who matches insult for insult will be seen as angry, sarcastic, and bitchy. Forget B. as well; you lose power and seem *defensive* if you let them critique your coiffure.

Try a *mirthful* variation of C. By making fun of the situation rather than counterattacking the heckler, you can bring a powerful—and distinctly female—response to the bantering arena. To do this, consider a variation on the old distinction between laughing *at* someone versus laughing *with*. Yes, he is trying to laugh at you; but laughing at him will only escalate the attack. When you counter with a comment about looking distinguished, you invite him to laugh *with* you at the *situation*, and you quickly shift the balance of power in your favor.

Managing verbal attacks from men that are disguised as humor can be a piece of work. You can begin by practicing what humor researchers call "humor as Aikido."

USING HUMOR AS A MARTIAL ART

The office was buzzing with word of a lucrative deal that broker Terry S., 33, had closed over dinner the previous evening. One of her male co-workers greeted her with a lewd smile, "Say, Terry, I heard you were working *real* late last night to close the Jameson deal." Terry's reply: "You know, Dan, I've never been able to figure out the right time to sleep with a client. If I did it before the deal closed, he might change his mind; and once he signs, why *would* I?" Dan laughed and congratulated her in a more genuine way.

Explains Terry: "If I had gotten angry, I would have given him ammunition—established his power. When the guys in the office start teasing in a sexual, hostile, or even silly way, I know I have three choices: I can join in the hostility, get defensive and try to prove how good I am, or I can joke and maintain my control of the moment."

Terry's powerful style is something that Dr. Joel Goodman, director of the Humor Project, would call the use of humor as Aikido. Goodman describes Aikido as the only Eastern martial art that doesn't involve offensive moves. Instead, it emphasizes a kind of harmony and moving with your attacker in a way that dissolves discord and avoids humiliating yourself or your opponent. It allows the person who opposes you to be subdued by the force of his or her own motion.

"If you were physically attacked," explains Goodman, "you would have three options: 1) you could fight back; you'd be standing up for yourself but running the risk of escalating the conflict; 2) you could be passive and allow yourself to be pushed against the wall–this might avoid a blowup, but you'd find fingerprints all over your face; or 3) you could go with the flow of the attack, holding your ground, pivoting as your attacker reaches you and sending him on his way."

For women at work, a verbal version of the skill of Aikido can create a distinctly female and powerful response to male humor, one that satirizes the situation.

MORE SITUATION COMEDY

When Terry joked about the mock dilemma of "when to sleep with a client," she resisted the impulse to attack Dan directly for his cutting commentary. She effectively rerouted the conversation with a confident and playful comment about the situation. In this way, she gracefully maneuvered her attacker and gained control of the moment.

At a recent presidential convention, the Women's Democratic Caucus offered an amusing application of situation comedy. When confronted with a sexist or patronizing comment on the floor of the convention, they simply handed the offending male a card that stated: "YOU HAVE JUST INSULTED A WOMAN."

Three other examples:

> Actress Eve Arden made fun of a practical joke when her male costar tried to sabotage her performance by arranging to have an unscheduled phone call ring loudly on stage. Instead of breaking character, she redirected the joke by picking up the phone and handing it to him, saying, "It's for you."

A new teacher was greeted on her first day of class by all of her students simultaneously sweeping their books from their desks onto the floor. Instead of lecturing them, she looked at her watch, swept the books from her desk, and said, "I guess I'm a little late, I thought we were doing it at 10:01!"

Janice B., 35, an attorney, was one of two women in an otherwise all male weekly staff meeting that always began with 10 minutes of sports talk in a deliberate attempt to exclude the women. After several polite moves to change the subject, Janice tried a rather outrageous—and successful—maneuver. In the midst of a verbal instant replay, she turned to her female colleague and inquired in a stage voice, "What kind of tampons do you use?" The men laughed, started the meeting, and refrained thereafter from postgame patter.

What all of these examples share in common is a sense of play. Even though the "attacking" person may have bared his teeth, each of these women responded in a way that said, "I know you are kidding." One woman described this process of getting in on the joke: "With humor, I get them to play on *my* team."

But a playful response takes practice. Let's say you are talking about returning to work after a maternity leave and a male colleague says, "What are you planning to do, set up a nursery in your office?" Quick—before you express your wish that *his* mother had used birth control —choose a more playful response.

WOULD YOU SAY:

A. "Don't be rude, Tom, I have day care all arranged when I come back to the job in January."

B. "I suppose you think that women belong at home with their babies."

C. "Well, actually, Tom, your office is a little more spacious; I thought I might set up a nursery in there."

Forget about A.; you have taken the bait and you sound both *aggressive* and silly. B. is the classic *defensive* response. Try C.; your *mirthful* comment satirizes the situation and demonstrates your confidence about returning to work.

In using humor as a martial art, your goal is to make fun of the situation, to "play" with the offending words or ideas. Women in politics are especially adept at these light-footed moves. Here are some classic comments from past campaigns.

"George Bush asked how I felt about the vice-presidency," reported Transportation Secretary Elizabeth Dole at a dinner roast (long before her husband, Bob, declared his candidacy in 1987). "I said, 'If you're interested in staying on, George, I'll keep you in mind.' "

> During Geraldine Ferraro's historic first day of campaigning for vice-president, she talked about blueberries with Mississippi Agricultural Commissioner Jim "Buck" Ross. "Can you bake blueberry muffins?" asked the courtly, 70-year-old Ross. "I think I can," said Ferraro. Then, smiling, she asked, "Can you?"

Plan to enlist techniques of silent comedy to help manage your inner response to macho office antics. When the insults and quips start flying, enjoy comic relief with a playful mental image that removes you from the stress of the moment. One accountant pictures the senior partners as little boys cheating at marbles; another woman pictures them dripping wet, snapping towels at one another in the locker room. Your own amusing images can keep you from a defensive, angry reply. When the joke is on you, quickly ask yourself: "What do these guys remind me of? Dogs in a kennel? Roosters in a cockfight? The Three Musketeers—or the Three Stooges?"

*T*ARGET *P*RACTICE: *R*ESPONDING TO *M*ALE *H*UMOR *W*ITHOUT *I*MITATING *I*T

Practice "situation comedy" with a playful response to the incidents described below. Remember, your response needn't result in uproarious laughter; the goal is for you to take a light-handed approach and hold your ground.

•••

PRACTICE

You arrive at work wearing your new Perry Ellis jacket. As you walk by his desk a male colleague asks, "Hey, where'd you get those shoulder pads–from the Green Bay Packers?" How can you block his kick–without tackling him?

   Hint: Try playing with the sports idea. You could say, "Yeah, I'm planning to go the whole nine yards with the Logan account today."

   What other approaches could you use?

PRACTICE

Your sales totals are down this quarter and a co-worker says, "What's the matter, Rita, lost your magic touch?" How might you respond with a light touch?

   Hint: Try a play on the "magic" angle. You could comment: "I should have never loaned my magic wand to *you*."

   What variations might work for you?

PRACTICE

You've been losing weight–a source of amusement and envy to your large-waisted colleagues. At staff meetings the men take turns urging you to have "just *one* donut." How might you lightly turn down the greasy offering?

   Hint: Try kidding about food. You can say, "No, thanks, I had a half-dozen maple bars for breakfast."

   What other comments could you make?

In her book *Sweet Success*, Kathleen Stechert writes about one woman's ability to roll with the punches. When she arrived in the office on Monday morning with a bandaged wrist (broken in a weekend softball game), one of her male co-workers asked, "What did you do, try to commit suicide?" This good-humored woman laughed and replied, "Yeah, it was the thought of working with you guys for one more week."

As you learn to "get in on the joke," you will feel increased comfort and competence in your relationships with men in the office. Your power will be the ability to playfully redefine situations, without resorting to the aggressive antics of men at work.

Is a sense of humor powerful enough to walk the high wire of sexual tension in the office? Let's take a closer look.

CHAPTER NINE

....

"THAT'S *NOT* FUNNY": HANDLING SEXUAL TENSION AT WORK

Q: How many women does it take to change a light bulb?

A: One, and that's *not* funny.

Sexual tension may be the last frontier for lightening up on the job. Whether the occasion is a gender jibe, a rude stare, or an obvious innuendo, his misdemeanor may leave you feeling wounded, humorless, even speechless. Yet you needn't be at a loss for words. In this chapter, you will discover that being a good-humored woman in moments of sexual tension is not a question of "selling out," being "one of the boys," or even being able to "take a joke." It is knowing how to point to the absurdity of the situation with a gentle jest.

BANTERING WITH THE *BOYS*: *TWO TECHNIQUES TO MANAGE SEXUAL TENSION*

Writer Kathleen Stechert offers this instructive scenario: At her firm's annual dinner, Donna L. was talking about her plans to finish her MBA at night school when David R. —a less-than-charming senior member—asked, "What are you going to do? Put a picture of yourself on your kid's bedroom door?" His snide remark brushed against Donna's own fears about being an absent parent. She responded by skipping dessert, excusing herself, and crying in the bathroom.

Consider, says Stechert, what would have happened if Donna had used humor to put his stinging remark in perspective. She might have said, for example, "No need, she's already got me on videotape," or "Is that what *you* do when you're out of town?" With these responses she could have lessened her vulnerability and coped more effectively. She would have discovered that the power of humor to control social situations is not for men only.

"I've learned how to banter with men, to tease them about their sexism," is the way Erin J., 41, a sales trainer, describes her approach. Recently, as she set up chairs for a meeting, the first man to arrive commented, "Isn't that just like a woman, always arranging the furniture." Says Erin, "I was determined not to respond to his comment as a challenge to my credibility, so I told him, 'If you like my decorating, wait until you taste my cooking!' He laughed and asked me about my agenda for the meeting."

The power in any situation at work lies in who defines it. When Erin responded to a sexist remark with a bantering reply, she defined the situation as a funny, not threatening, one. Try the following two techniques to manage sexual tension by bantering with the boys in the office.

MIRRORING

Let's practice using the technique of mirroring (see Chapter 6) to tackle the "terms of endearment" problem. It's hard to be effective with the sounds of "honey," "cookie," or "girlie" ringing in your ears. You don't want to be heavy-handed, but these terms reduce your credibility and make you sound small and silly. Here are two examples of how the technique of mirroring (simply mimicking or playing with the patronizing comment) can educate the offending gentleman.

> Elizabeth M., an accountant, was at a lunch with Robert, 42, a longtime client, who insistently referred to her as "Liz" and "Lizzie" throughout the meal. She made her point when she began to call him "Bobby." Several "Bobbys" later, he said, "Oh, you like to be called Elizabeth, don't you?"

> Claire V. had just completed an outstanding client presentation. As her boss walked her down the hall, he "complimented" her, saying, "Not bad, for a girl." Claire was speechless at the time; but her chance came later that month. Following her boss's speech to a professional group, she commented, "Not bad, for a boy." After a moment of shock, he laughed. This exchange became a standing joke between them.

In each case, the patronizing comment was managed by mirroring the male speaker's metaphor. By listening for the image in his comment and playing with it, each woman was able to maintain her power and poise while gently educating the man in question. Once again, the object is directing your humor to the situation. Women won't succeed with locker-room, towel-snapping insults. Avoid blaming and ridiculing by mirroring and slightly exaggerating his point of view.

If a male colleague asks, "What are you girls doing today?" don't punish him with a blistering chorus of "I Am Woman." Instead, build on his image with a jesting version of what "girls" do. You can answer, "We girls thought we would play a few hands of bridge, have some chicken salad, and tackle the budget projections."

So the next time a client or co-worker calls you "Hon," don't lecture him; try a more pithy punchline: "Hon? Why don't you call me by my real name: Attila."

Are you wasting time fuming about being asked to do things that are not in your job description? You've read the fine print and there is nothing in your contract about making coffee or taking notes during a meeting. So when you are asked to make coffee, other than adding a teaspoon of salt to each cup, what are your choices?

DO YOU SAY:

A. "Do I look like Mrs. Olson?"

B. "I'll make the coffee, but my time bills at fifty dollars an hour. It will be a five-dollar cup of coffee."

C. (Pulling a coin out of your pocket) "I'll flip you for it."

Avoid A.; it's too *aggressive* and sarcastic, and comparing yourself to a television pitchwoman who wears a braided chignon is not conducive to your credibility. In B., citing your salary is a *defensive* ploy and makes you sound like you take yourself and your time too seriously. Instead, try C., a *mirthful* response; it makes fun of the situation and avoids a focus on you or your chauvinistic colleague.

Humor that mirrors or playfully mocks the situation is the best tactic to handle patronizing, stereotypical comments. Your response may be like Linda's:

> Linda S., 35, a banker, had just concluded a business meeting with her boss and a client. As the client prepared to leave, he reached into his briefcase for a novelty item he customarily gave to suppliers: a small plastic paper cutter. He presented one to Linda's boss, saying, "John, this is perfect for clipping articles from *The Wall Street Journal*." Turning to Linda, he said, "Here, dear, you'll love this for clipping recipes." "Thank you, George," Linda replied. "I'll use it the next time I see a recipe in *The Wall Street Journal*."

Faced with a sarcastic or scalding lecture, most men become defensive and fail to learn from the situation. If you invite him to look in the mirror and see the silliness in his comment, you may render the office dinosaur extinct.

THE "AS IF" PLOY

Plan to use your sense of humor as a secret weapon when you encounter more overt hostility. The key here is responding to remarks *"as if"* the speaker is joking. By employing the *"as if"* strategy, you maintain control; your good humor becomes a way of saying, "This isn't insulting, it's funny." Listen to two good-humor women using this strategy:

> Valerie C. was a newly hired radio personality at a southern station. Her immediate supervisor wore his chauvinism like a

badge, greeting her arrival every day with such shopwork classics as "Women belong at home with their kids," and "Why do you want to take this job away from a man who needs it?" Valerie responded by taking his comments lightly and offering a bantering commentary on his remarks: "You're just saying that to impress me," she would say, or "Say, *that's* a new one." Within several weeks, his comments stopped.

Mavis was the sole female executive in a Los Angeles record company. During an all-male client dinner, her boss turned to her and loudly asked, "Mavis, what kind of lingerie turns you on?" She deftly replied, "Boxer shorts." Still he persisted, "But, really, what turns women on?" Mavis' smiling answer won her the respect of every man at the table: "Just by being yourself, Michael."

USING LIGHTNESS TO SET LIMITS

At a women's conference, a participant stood up and told an appalling story. She was meeting with her boss, who was talking about what he'd like to have for lunch: "I'd like something with lots of protein, something I can eat at my desk. Any suggestions?" She thought and answered, "How about peanut butter?" Her boss smiled and said, "If I can smear it all over you."

The woman left the room speechless, cheeks burning. Her boss's comment was totally out of character, and for weeks she wondered how she might have brushed the remark aside. From our distance, let's consider her choices. Should she have said:

A. "Would that be creamy or crunchy?"

B. "How dare you? That's disgusting!"

C. "I thought you wanted a sandwich, not a fetish."

A. is a mistake because it builds on the sexual innuendo; B. focuses on the invitation. C. highlights the absurdity of his comment and provides an ideal exit line.

Your sense of lightness is the best way to put distance between yourself and the client more interested in pleasure than business. When a man puts his hand on your thigh, spare him your sexual code of honor ("I never sleep with clients," followed by the world's oldest lie, "but I'm flattered"). Judy B., a corporate vice-president, finds it more politic–and effective–to say simply, "I think your hand is lost." Michelle V., an underwriter, closes the subject in a firm and funny way: "What, and destroy *both* of our fantasies?"

While it is best to avoid humiliating the would-be Lothario, there are situations where it is more important to your credibility to let your colleagues know that this fellow is not "coming up to see you sometime."

Vicki S. was the only woman at a sales conference meeting. Wayne R., the chair of the meeting, relished his reputation as a "traveling salesman," and throughout the meeting he looked at Vicki pointedly and said, "I know how to handle a woman."

Although Vicki didn't want to embarrass Wayne in front of his peers, she decided it was more important to let her co-workers know that he wasn't going to handle *her.* When the meeting closed after dark, Vicki said, "Well, Wayne, since you know how to handle a woman, you'll probably want to call your wife before you leave the building."

That meeting was two years ago. Vicki tells me her comment made her a legend in the company. "I still have guys coming up to me and saying, 'Way to go, Vicki, you really put Wayne in his place.' "

Outrageous humor will short-circuit outrageous behavior, but you'll want to consider whether the consequences of your comedy are worth the risk. Esther C., an advertising copywriter, was sitting in a meeting when she noticed that a colleague had his eyes fixed firmly on her breasts. Later that morning he asked her a question and she refused to reply. Undaunted and still eyeing her anatomy, he asked, "What's the matter, didn't you hear my question?" Esther's response stopped the seminar cold: "Yes, I heard you," she answered, "but *they* don't talk."

We might argue the merits of Esther's richly deserved retort. The problem is that she not only publicly ridiculed a colleague but she also focused even more attention on her body. Ideally, she might have confronted him alone and, assuming he continued to stare, simply lifted his chin until his eyes reached to her eye level.

THREE QUESTIONS TO SKEWER SEXISM

Don't worry about being witty; sometimes a simple question can deflect an outrageous remark. You'll be able

to use these three questions in countless situations:
1) *"What makes you say that?"* 2) *"Why do you ask?"*
3) *"Would you repeat that?"* Each of these deflectors gives
you the power to end an inappropriate conversation.

> **He:** You're pretty disagreeable today. Is it "that"
> time of the month?
>
> **She:** *What makes you say that?*
>
> **He:** How come an attractive woman like you
> doesn't have a boyfriend?
>
> **She:** *Why do you ask?*
>
> **He:** You've just been dying to go to bed with me!
>
> **She:** *Would you repeat that?*

PUTTING MIRTH TO WORK

Mirth can work to dissolve sexual tensions on the job. The
key is practice and knowing how and when to use it.
Remember to evaluate each occasion. Laughter has its
limits; distinguish between sexual heckling and sexual
harassment. His comments may be patronizing and
annoying, but are they amenable to your laughter and
his? A good-humored approach works best to introduce a
problem or serve as a non-nagging reminder. But is his
hand on your knee habitual? Is his needling abusive or
reflected on your performance appraisal? If so, your
approach must be documentation, confrontation, and
perhaps even a job change.

Don't forget the power of silent comedy. Enjoying a
momentary mental image can offer quick comic relief. As
you pause to think of an image, you become an observer of
the situation. From this distance you are less likely to be
angry, defensive, or aggressive. So picture the offending
gentleman as Howard the Duck or Prince Valiant, or mentally replay the theme music from *Jaws* as he walks away.

One CPA likes to picture her overbearing boss as the Wizard of Oz in the scene where Toto reveals the Wizard's deception. She pictures her boss saying, "Pay no attention to that man behind the curtain!"

JEST FOR SUCCESS

Sharpen your wits by planning a light-handed yet authoritative response to the following situations. Remember, it doesn't matter if he laughs; your goal is to maintain control of the situation by defining it in your terms.

PRACTICE

Your supervisor always greets you at your monthly review meeting by saying, "So, good-looking, how's it going?" How might you break his nasty habit—without being heavy-handed?

Hint: Try a play on words that mirrors or mimics the expression "good-looking." You could answer, "Well, my *sales figures* are looking good."

What other variations will work for you?

PRACTICE

You've just returned from a successful speech at your professional association's state meeting. A male colleague asks, "How did your 'little' presentation go?" How can you expand his small mind, without being preachy?

Hint: Try joking about his patronizing choice of words. You might say, "I wish it *had* been little; there was a crowd of five hundred. But it was great to hear all of those hands clapping."

What other approaches could you use?

PRACTICE

You are the only woman present when a personnel hiring discussion begins to sound like a *Playboy* centerfold selection. How might you lightly reroute the conversation?

Hint: Try making fun of the situation: You could look at your watch and say, "My schedule must be wrong, I thought the hiring meeting was at ten and the stag party was at eleven."

What other comments might work for you?

With practice, you'll be prepared with similar comebacks for all occasions. I remember the one Ella Grasso, then governor of Connecticut, prepared when, after much controversy, she was the first woman to speak to the all-male Gridiron Club in Washington, D.C. Following a flowery introduction from her male host, Grasso looked out at the assembled men and began: "And to think that I gave up a Tupperware party to come here this evening."

PART FIVE

BRINGING IT
ALL BACK HOME

CHAPTER TEN

··

HUMOR ON THE
HOME FRONT

*S*heila D., 33, an exhausted manager of a personnel firm, arrived at home on an evening when her family was expected at her parents' house for dinner. As she opened the front door, she snarled her greeting: "Why isn't everybody ready to leave?" Her husband, sense of humor intact, looked at his watch, smiled, and said, "Excuse me, I was expecting my wife right about now; did you happen to see her in the driveway?" Sheila laughed, did an about-face, walked out the front door and in again, this time greeting her family with good humor.

LAUGHING ALL THE WAY HOME: FOUR TECHNIQUES TO BRING LIGHTNESS HOME FROM THE OFFICE

How can we avoid this arsenic hour when we first get home? How can we bring laughter and lightness home from the office? You may have managed your office with wit and wisdom; but does the day's end leave you frowning, haunted by problems, berating yourself for mistakes? When someone asks, "How was your day?" do you tell them...and tell them? Do you greet loved ones by quaffing two martinis and slipping into a semi-coma of self-involvement?

Think of lightening up as a total state of mind, one that can carry your good humor beyond the office door. In this chapter, we'll highlight mirthful techniques for unwinding from work and for moving closer to the ones you love. The beauty of your sense of humor away from the office is that you can safely experiment with more intimate, and sometimes sillier, kinds of humor.

Let's start with four techniques to practice on the way home to turn the lights back on and allow you to enjoy friends and family after work.

MAKE COMIC COMPARISONS

On your way home, ask yourself some of the "Barbara Walters questions" suggested as silent comedy in Chapter 4. Reconnect with your sense of lightness by reconsidering the people and problems of the day as comic metaphors. Ask yourself: What does this troublesome situation or person remind me of? The answer will provide a comic distancing perspective about the day's pressures and the opportunity to leave them behind.

- What kind of bread does my company or office remind me of?
  Hint: (bagel, Wonder bread, oat-bran)

- Think of a problematic situation in the office and ask: Which soup does this client or project resemble?
  Hint: (chicken noodle, clam chowder, cream of broccoli)

- Pick an obnoxious boss or customer from your day and determine: Which bumper sticker best expresses his or her philosophy or personality?
  Hint: ("I brake for no one!" "S.O.B. on board!")

I couldn't survive without comic comparisons. A favorite of mine involves Lucille Ball as a comic muse. Whenever my day has included rushing to make a plane connection, meeting a writing or a client project deadline, I picture myself in one particular episode of "I Love Lucy," standing with Lucy and Ethel Mertz on the assembly line of that wacky candy factory. The candies are coming out faster and faster; we are stuffing them into our mouths and our pockets and purses. Just when we get caught up, the supervisor calls out, "You're doing great; let's *speed the line up!*"

My husband, an architect, is a recent convert to the art of silent comedy. As Jeremy tells it: "You know, that silent comedy stuff really works. Before I came home today, I was waiting for over an hour in the building department. By the time I left, I was fuming; but just before I walked out, I looked around the waiting room and thought: Maybe this wasn't the building department after all, maybe I wandered into a casting call for a Fellini movie!"

PRACTICE

Pause on the way home to reconsider the office follies as a source of material for: a soap opera ("The Old and Righteous"), a situation comedy ("One Day at a Dime"), or a headline for a tabloid newspaper ("UFO Steals Budget Memo").

TAKE A LIGHTER VIEW

Carrying your good humor home from work is not simply a laughing matter; it is the practice of creating distance from the day's events. In the words of an ancient Chinese proverb: "You cannot stop the bird of sorrow from flying over your head; but you can keep him from making a nest in your hair."

• •

Consider how Geri P., 44, program director for a professional association, practices this art. "At the end of the day I can always tell when I have lost my perspective. I fall into what I call my 'stinking thinking'—I see everything as negative, as my fault. I feel overwhelmed, out of control, a victim. It's taken me years to learn the secret of lightening up to enjoy the ride and know that eventually I will solve the problem."

Does Geri's "stinking thinking" sound all too familiar? Your friends and family may need to duck for cover when you come home if your thoughts about on-the-job trauma travel down one of these three dark roads:

- *Do you personalize the incident?* ("I really blew it!" "How could I have been so stupid?" "What's wrong with me?")

- *Do you generalize about the outcome?* ("This always happens!" "I'll never get the hang of it!")

- *Do you catastrophize about the future?* ("Now I'll never land the contract!" "Now it's all going to fall apart!" "What if my boss finds out?")

Instead of burning yourself at the stake, try three questions that take a lighter (and ultimately more professional view) of the day's negatives.

PRACTICE

Summon a less-than-successful scenario from your day. 1) Instead of asking, "How could I have been so stupid?" ask: *"What did I learn?"* 2) Instead of lamenting, "This always happens," ask: *"What can I do next time?"* 3) Instead of predicting, "It's all going to fall apart!" ask: *"What can I do tomorrow?"*

TRY MY GRANDMOTHER'S THEORY OF RELATIVITY

As a teenager, my grandmother Rachel was a young revolutionary in Czarist Russia whose idea of a date was to sneak into the soldiers' camp with her boyfriend and talk against the reign of Czar Nicholas. She visited often during my whining, teenage years, when she could enrage my sisters and me by uttering a simple Yiddish phrase. Whenever we would complain to her about a teacher, a class project, or a boyfriend, she would smile and say, *"Shana-Rayna-Kapora"*—which by then we knew meant, "It could have been worse."

I found the concept infuriating in those years, but recently, on a trip to Los Angeles, my sister Mavis reminded me of the potential power of my grandmother's sense of relativity. I was on the last stop of a grueling book tour for *Leaving the Office Behind* and I was scheduled to appear on CNN's NEWSNIGHT for a 30-minute interview and call-in show. I had watched the show once and found the hosts amiable and nonconfrontive. However, during my appearance they metamorphosed into piranhas—jabbing, needling, and arguing with all my answers. I maneuvered through the interview and returned to my hotel flattened and exhausted.

Just as I was finishing all of the chocolate in my hotel room's mini-bar, my sister Mavis called. "Barbara, you handled them beautifully," she said—all sisterly support. "Maybe," I whined, "but they were just awful." Said Mavis, *"Shana-Rayna-Kapora;* it could have been worse. You didn't get angry, you didn't cry, you didn't throw up!"

We cackled into our phones, and the interview became a part of my comic history.

PRACTICE

List one or more of this week's Maalox moments (a slide projector jammed; you forgot a client's name; your project ran over budget). Repeat the phrase, *"Shana-Rayna-Kapora"* and ask yourself: How could it have been worse? Consider the most slapstick, absurd, exaggerated extension of the moment; don't stop until you are laughing.

Take the time on your way home to create a theory of relativity about the unfinished or ill-fated events in the office. Here are some theories I've heard:

> *From a small business owner:* "I want to live to enjoy the fruits of my business succeeding. So I remind myself, if one deal goes down, we'll get another."

> *From an advertising executive:* "I posted a note above my desk in the office and I read it before I leave for home. It says, 'We are not doing brain surgery here.'"

> *From a corporate vice-president:* "The young son of our CEO died of leukemia, so whenever I get overly serious about something, I remind myself that nothing that happens in the office is a matter of life and death."

> *From an administrator:* "I have worked thirty-two years in this company, and if I make a mistake, I kid myself on the way home: What do you expect for your first day on the job?"

CELEBRATE AND CONGRATULATE

Remember, too, that the lighter view is not simply dealing with what disgraced former Vice-President Spiro Agnew once called the "nattering nabobs of negativity." Traveling light also means recognizing and celebrating victories. The best time to do this is by yourself on the way home (since only your immediate colleagues can understand the intricacies of your latest brilliant maneuver).

Pause on the way home to acknowledge the triumphs, great and small (you finessed a problem with a customer or co-worker, the client loved your ideas, your budget is taking shape, you got your PC to do what you wanted it to). Sit back and envision the larger meaning behind the small—and sometimes teeth-gnashing—details of your job (that your work contributes an important product or service to your community, for example).

PRACTICE

List three successes you can savor. What did you do? What was the impact? How did it make a difference in the life of your company, client, customer, community? Give yourself a standing ovation.

LAUGHTER IS THE CLOSEST DISTANCE BETWEEN TWO PEOPLE: FOUR FUNNY WAYS TO DEFUSE CONFLICT

The Bushmen of the Kalahari Desert have a unique ritual of divorce: When one partner wants to dissolve the union, he or she simply dismantles the family hut. But consider the way one couple ended their "divorce proceedings." In the midst of a long, loud argument, the husband began to angrily remove the palm leaves from the top of the thatched hut. He worked rapidly, moving leaves to the ground until he suddenly paused, realizing the significance of his action. He looked helplessly at his wife, who responded by picking up one of the fallen leaves, dusting it off, and saying, "What a good idea; these leaves need to be shaken."

This wonderful story reminds me of how quickly lightness de-escalates problems between loved ones, creating what sociologist Irving Goffman calls "a change in the situational frame." I remember driving home from dinner at a relative's house with Jeremy. I was complaining about the controlling behavior of a family member, and Jeremy started to defend him. The conversation escalated into an argument; we drove faster and argued louder. Suddenly I realized we were both tense from the evening and I saw how unimportant the argument was. I leaned over, touched Jeremy's shoulder, and melodramatically asked: "Can this marriage be saved?"

The art of comic containment in loving relationships will require a combination of self-control and practice, practice, practice. Try three funny ways to control the climate and resume closeness with lovers, friends, and family.

USE ACTION-STOPPING PHRASES

Maureen A. had just introduced her older sister Betty to her newly beloved boyfriend, Edward. Maureen called Betty the next day and Betty began to recite a grocery list of things that were wrong with Edward. Said Betty: "He seems so insecure and macho; no wonder he's never been married. And why hasn't he passed his law boards yet? I also noticed that he drank more than anyone at the table." Answered Maureen (who knew how judgmental Betty could be): "Don't hold back, Betty, tell me what you really think!" Betty laughed and said, "I'm sorry; I guess I just feel so protective of you."

Practice using action-stopping phrases that help make molehills out of mountains. Depending on the circumstance, you might say, for example:

"Are we having fun yet?"

"Would you like to dance?"

"This is sure more fun than making love."

"Should my attorney call your attorney?"

SHARE SILENT COMEDY

Mike and Greta M.'s fathers were a study in contrasts: Mike's father was a fair-haired, squash-playing bank executive; cool, calm, collected—not the least bit comic. Greta's father was a handsome, dark-eyed entrepreneur, a successful man with a genuine fondness for dicey jokes and saucy stories. In the middle of their annual post-Christmas argument (*Mike:* "Your father is so crude." *Greta:* "Your father is so up-tight"), Greta started laughing hysterically. "What's so funny?" demanded Mike. Said Greta, "I just had the funniest image: One of my father's dirty jokes coming out of your father's pristine mouth!" Mike joined the laughter; her image had ended the argument.

If you have been practicing throughout the book, you have developed savvy and skill in the art of comic comparison. The trick in a crisis is to stop, share what you are seeing, and invite the other person to dance in the light. Choose a movie, book, television show, or popular song that you have shared with your partner, parent, or friend, and use it as a refreshing reference point. For instance, a married couple who watch "Dallas": "We sound like J.R.

and Sue Ellen before their second divorce." Two friends or lovers who saw the movie *The Odd Couple*: "I'm so messy and you're so neat; we're like Oscar and Felix." With these comparisons, you stop the action and lightly lower the thermostat.

Don't forget the power of cartoons to convey a message. Posting a cartoon with the message, "This reminds me of our conversation (or situation)," is a marvelous way to reestablish equilibrium with friends and family.

MAKE FUN OF THE SITUATION

Stephanie S. was on a second date with a charming man who had just finished serving her an elegant dinner in his apartment. He cleared the dishes and asked her if she wanted coffee and brandy. She did, and he disappeared into the kitchen, reappearing 10 minutes later, completely nude, with drinks and coffee on a silver tray. Said Stephanie with a smile: "I see you brought something to stir the drinks with."

As Stephanie demonstrated, sometimes the best exit from a ticklish situation is simply to make fun of the situation itself. I laugh every time I remember the scene from Larry McMurtry's book *Terms of Endearment*, where the daughter tells her mother that she is pregnant. When her mother fails to respond with delight, daughter says, "If you are not going to be happy for me, I'm going to be very mad!" Her vain and self-absorbed mother explodes: "Happy? Why should I be happy about being old enough to be a grandmother?" The daughter's husband, who is watching the fireworks, mildly asks his mother-in-law: "Does this mean you won't be knitting us any baby booties?"

We had some fun with the "Does this mean" formula in Chapter 5, and now you'll be able to use it to allow humor to blossom in close relationships. Listen as Audrey R., 57, an advertising executive, describes a dinner with a man she was dating. He was unusually silent and she remarked, "You seem quiet tonight; is anything wrong?" He responded with an irritable non sequitur: "I just don't want to get involved right now." Gamely she replied, "Does that mean I shouldn't order dessert?"

CREATE HAPPIER ENDINGS

Sharpen your skill by planning a light and loving response to the following situations. Your goal is to allow humor to create a temporary cease-fire.

PRACTICE

You are in the midst of a raging argument with your husband about your son's grades. How might you close the gap in the conversation?

Hint: Try a comic comparison. You could say, "We really are stuck here. I can't help but wonder: What would Ward and June Cleaver have done in this situation?"

What other variations will work for you?

PRACTICE

You are having a political argument with a friend that has progressed from a discussion of the issues to attacking each other's basic political values. How can you stop the caucus before it undermines your friendship?

Hint: Try an action-stopping phrase. For example: "It always amazes me how much we agree about these things!" or "So, now that we have convinced each other, let's talk about something else."

What other approach might work here?

You have just poked the pot roast and determined that it is on the rare side. Your omnipresent mother-in-law or know-it-all pal warns, "You'd better take it out or it will be like leather." You start to simmer and say, "Listen, I've made a roast hundreds of times; *I* know when it's done!" How can you back down—without getting burned?

Hint: Try making fun of the situation. For example: You might laugh and ask, "Did I say I've made hundreds of pot roasts? I meant millions!" or "Does this mean you don't want yours well done?"

What else might you say?

Your loving good humor is a question of both action and attitude. A lighter touch can even change long-standing patterns in love and romance. Perhaps your situation will be like Julia's, who had a long, unhappy romantic history.

> Julia A., 33, moved swiftly through a series of painful affairs, confirming her negative view of men as cold and unable to make a commitment. In time, she was able to take a lighter view as she learned to look for vital clues—a process she jokingly referred to as her resolution to "never go out on a second date with a man who was: married, never married and over 35, divorced less than six months, ordered double martinis at lunch, or brought his son on a first date."

When she began to allow herself to enjoy the company of emotionally available men, Julia was able to alter her negative expectations and eventually form a close bond with a warm and attractive man. Developing her sense of lightness lifted her bitter veil so she was able to recognize a dear man when she met him.

NAGGING VERSUS JESTING: TWO WAYS TO STOP NAGGING AND START JESTING

"Grumbling," said the sensuous Marlene Dietrich, "is the death of romance." The Blue Angel is right, of course; but how can you discuss unsexy subjects (like dirty dishes, wayward socks, overbearing attitudes, or overtime at the office)? Suggests Alex G., 34, "I use humor as a way of introducing tough topics or as a reminder when I don't want a full-scale confrontation—when I'm not ready to go to the mat. If I am less heavy, the subject loses some of its importance. When I can approach it in a lighthearted way, I get rid of the attitude that I've got to win."

I think you'll be tickled by the triumph of jesting over nagging in Sylvia's relationship with her husband. Sylvia R., 39, is a home manager and mother of two, whose husband is an executive vice-president of a large corporation. After enduring months of her husband working barricaded in his study after dinner, she said, "David, I'd like to have one night a week with you, and if you bring your briefcase home tomorrow night I'm going to toss it in the pool." The next night, of course, David "forgot" and brought the briefcase home. Sylvia intercepted him at the front door and tossed it into the pool. Said Sylvia, "I never knew my husband could walk on water!"

Sylvia assured me that nothing inside the case was damaged and that the incident finally initiated a caring conversation and some reasonable compromises about

working at home. She also posted a lighthearted reminder in his study–a cartoon of a woman at a perfume
counter, saying, "My husband is a workaholic–do you
have any perfume that smells like a desk?"

Try two ways of tackling tough topics–without using
an iron fist.

IMITATE EACH OTHER

"For weeks my husband had been coming home in high
gear," recalls Emily H., 32. "He would walk through the
door and start ordering the kids and me around like we
were his secretary and staff. I tried to talk to him about it,
but he said I was being overly sensitive. Then one night,
after he had changed clothes and positioned himself in
front of the nightly news, I went upstairs, put on his suit
jacket and grabbed his briefcase. I slipped out of the back
door and let myself in the front door, doing a great imitation of him–shouting orders, being obnoxious. He
laughed and asked, 'Do I really do that?' We all nodded
'yes.' Now whenever he starts to act this way, I ask him, 'Do
you want me to go and put on your jacket?' "

Imitation is the silliest–and often most effective–
form of humor in close relationships. It offers a loved one
a zany, rather than angry, opportunity to examine his or
her behavior without becoming defensive. The laughter is
a giant step in the direction of change.

For one couple, imitation can short-circuit an argument; for another, imitation lightens a heavy conversation about the office. Explains Jill D., 43: "Tom and I have
developed a special signal: When a discussion is getting
out of hand, one of us will cool the conversation by saying,
'Would you like me to show you what you look like/sound
like?' We stop and imitate each other, and we always end
up laughing."

Alicia G., 34, describes her husband's way of interrupt-
ing her when she is offering an oh-so-serious catalog of

horrors in her office. "First he listens to me and then cheers me up in an instant by imitating other people laughing: Eddie Murphy, Woody Woodpecker, Peewee Herman..."

For Kathleen and Wally N., a great imitation became a way to begin negotiating the war between the plates. Kathleen, 47, a public relations executive, arrived home from a grueling day and was greeted by a sinkful of dirty breakfast dishes with a sign in her husband's handwriting that said: "WASH ME." Wally left early the next morning. When he returned that evening, he found that Kathleen had papered the house with notes: on the oven door, "CLEAN ME"; on the bathtub, "SCRUB ME"; over the laundry basket, "FOLD ME." He was still smiling when she got home, and as a result they sat down and had a constructive conversation about the division of labor in their household.

CULTIVATE INSIDE JOKES

In her feisty memoir, *Pentimento*, Lillian Hellman wrote about her 30-year love affair with writer Dashiell Hammett. She offered a glimpse of how she poked fun at his patronizing manner, creating a long-standing inside joke. She wrote:

> I don't know if I was paying him back for his casual ladies of our early years...but certainly I was serious or semi-serious about another man....I told Dash that I had decided not to marry the man....
>
> [He said] "I would never have allowed that....It would never have been any good. The day it is good for you, I'll allow it."
>
> "Thank you," I said, "but if that happens, I won't ask for your permission....
>
> "Without my permission you won't ever do it."...

> For years after I would say such things
> as, "May I have your permission this morn-
> ing to go the hairdresser, then to the library,
> and on my way home buy an ice cream
> cone?"

Inside jokes create warm reminders, a kind of short-hand to gently remind each other of past follies, all too human flaws, and to help us communicate clearly in the present. Frances R., 43, was golfing with her husband, Howard, in Palm Springs. On the sixth hole she took out a three iron, and he said, "Use the five iron." She disagreed, but he persisted. Suddenly this argument was interrupted by the sound of two birds chirping loudly in a nearby Palo Verde bush. Said Frances to Howard, "He is probably trying to tell her which worm to eat." From that point on, when either Frances or Howard was being overbearing, the other partner would ask: "Are you trying to tell me which worm to eat?"

PRACTICE

Think of a recent clash with a loved one. How might the art of imitation have changed the encounter? Picture an argument or misunderstanding with a parent or partner; how might you now shape the scenario into a shared inside joke?

Two Caveats

Jesting has its limits. It is most effective as a playful way to open dialogue about a troubled topic, to short-circuit an argument, or serve as a gentle, non-nagging reminder. Explains Pamela R., 39, "I find humor in my house works in the short term, but not always in the long term. When my partner hasn't taken out the garbage or changed the towels, I will deflect things to our cat or to an imaginary clean-up crew, saying, 'Maybe Mallomar will take out the garbage,' or 'Will you remind the maid to put away your socks?' or 'It's a good thing the elves are coming tonight.' I sometimes can get a response from him on *that* day, but I know that we may have to have a more serious focused conversation before some things can change."

Remember that too much humor can be as heavy a burden as too little. "My boyfriend is always joking," complains Stella G., 32. "He tries to keep our conversation light. I wish just once I could get him to stop joking." The nonstop humor that Stella describes is a sign of her boyfriend's discomfort with intimate feelings. She would be wise to address her concern directly, saying, "I really love your sense of humor, but I need to know that we can talk seriously, too." Her message is that humor, in a relationship, is a seasoning that tastes best as a complement to other tastes.

As you survey the possibilities of loving good humor, perhaps the best model is the fictional character of the smart, savvy Nora Charles, played by Myrna Loy in *The Thin Man* movies. Loy invested Nora with a sly but loving sense of humor; she knew when to nurture or confront husband Nick Charles (played by William Powell) and also how to get him to do precisely what she wanted him to do without nagging (for example, the scene in *After the Thin Man*, when she persuades him to get up in the middle of the night and make her scrambled eggs). A recent tribute to the actress by The American Humorist Society featured a musical number by Cynthia Heimel offering this whimsical wisdom: "When in doubt, act like Myrna Loy."

*C*HAPTER *E*LEVEN

....

LIGHT
PARENTING

*L*ue-Rachelle B., 43, is encouraging her children to write a book called "When I grow up, I won't make *my* kids…" The manuscript grows weekly: whenever she asks them to do anything and they resist, she suggests they do the task and write it up in the book. Typical entries include: "When I grow up, I won't make my kids do the dinner dishes, clean their rooms on Saturday, be in bed by nine." In this marvelous way, she defuses the tension surrounding the power struggle that begins the moment a child is old enough to make his own bed.

In a similar light, one father handles his kids' nagging by inviting them to write their complaints on a "Saturday List." If this situation is not an emergency, it lands on the list. On Saturday morning he sits down with them and goes over every grievance, one by one. "Nine times out of ten," he says, "they will have forgotten it by then."

This chapter's lessons in lightness are an opportunity to nurture the developing sense of humor in your child's life—as well as offering comic relief from the family circus.

*W*HAT *K*IDS *F*IND *F*UNNY

At several months, many babies are laughing; by age four some children laugh several hundred times a day. But, as you have probably discovered, toddlers and teenagers find humor in very different things. Fascinating research by Dr. Robert Valett of California State University suggests that parents who use humor at home are wise to consider what tickles the funny bone as the child's sense of humor matures. Among the funny phases he has described:

1. Preschool Pranksters (ages 1–5): *You'll see slapstick, giggling, nonsense words, and nursery rhymes. At this age, noises from the body bring down the house.*

2. Middle Childhood Comics (ages 6–9): *Watch for practical jokes, playing around, obvious answers to silly questions ("I'm glad I'm not a fish." Why? " 'Cause I can't swim!").*

3. Late Childhood Riddler (ages 9–12): *The capacity for abstract thinking gives way to riddles and jokes that make you groan, such as knock-knock and elephant jokes—all told with great relish.*

4. Teenage Word Play (ages 12–14): *Be prepared for puns and jokes that play on various word meanings. Get ready to hear that your headache is all in your mind.*

5. Adolescent/Adult Satire (ages 15 and older): *Listen for more biting humor and anecdotes that come with growth of logic, judgment, and facility with language. Be prepared to be the butt of the joke.*

You can nurture a healthy sense of humor at all stages of your child's life: make funny faces at your baby; laugh at her knock-knock jokes (no matter how corny); take him to funny movies; laugh with her at situation comedy on TV; buy funny books for her birthday presents (anything by Dr. Seuss, Shel Silverstein, Judith Viorst's *Alexander and the Terrible, Horrible, No Good, Very Bad Day*, or Gary Larson's *Far Side* cartoon collections for teens).

Discourage kids from using put-down, racist, or sexist humor. To a younger child you can explain, "This isn't funny because it hurts when you make fun of someone's color, or their church, or about being a girl." With an older child, your response can be more straightforward: "I'm not laughing because I think that jokes at someone else's expense are hurtful and not funny."

Helping your child to see the lighter side of life offers rich rewards as a parent. But you'll also need to develop your own sense of humor to walk the front lines of life at home.

THE COMEDY OF COOPERATION: TWO PLAYFUL PATHS TO COOPERATION AND COMMUNICATION

Annette G., 39, has never been able to read a map, and on more than one occasion her "shortcuts" have driven her kids crazy. So whenever her three preteen kids are whining in the back seat en route to a movie, a friend's house, or a school dance, she keeps them in line with a laughable threat: "If you don't stop whining back there, I'm going to take a *shortcut*!"

Like Annette, you may have already found that humor is a special way to communicate with your kids and—just as important—to gain their cooperation and attention at home. Does the sight of a mound of your daughter's gym clothes elevate your blood pressure? Is your son's bedtime a nightmare? Do the frequent fights between your kids threaten your sanity? Does the music of Bon Jovi sound like fingernails on a blackboard? Try two playful solutions to cope with the problems at hand.

SPEAK IN UNDERSTATEMENT OR OVERSTATEMENT

Lois B., 41, had been trying to avoid the role of the wicked stepmother for a year since her marriage to Rich. But after many dead-end conversations, Matt's room continued to be a candidate for a Board of Health inspection. As a last resort, she walked into his room and said, "You know, Matt, I've decided that I don't care if you sleep on the floor; all I ask is that you change the sheets every six months or so." Several hours after her understatement, Matt walked to the washing machine with his dirty sheets.

With a similar technique, Dorothy R., 45, used overstatement to declare a truce between her two sons, ages eight and nine. "I felt like they had been fighting since sunrise," recalls Dorothy, "so I locked them in their dad's study with instructions not to come out until they kissed each other on the cheek and said, 'I love you, brother.' They must have been in there for two hours! But when they came out, they weren't fighting, and I haven't heard a fight for weeks. And if I see a fight coming, I'm going to ask them if they want to go to dad's study again."

USE THEIR LANGUAGE/ USE ANOTHER LANGUAGE

Nina K.'s head was beginning to feel like she was wearing a helmet that was too tight. All of her attempts to silence her three kids' shouting at the family dinner table had failed. Out of desperation, she caught their attention with a word that was not part of her usual vocabulary. "All right, you DWEEBS," she shouted, her voice rising above her three noisy children, "stop the screaming!" She was rewarded by their shocked faces, laughter, and reduced volume for the remainder of the meal.

When you borrow the language of your children to gain attention or cooperation, your effectiveness will depend on whether your humor suits their age. For example, parents of younger kids report great results from simply imitating the annoying acts. One mom announces an unpopular decision to her five-year-old, says, "Okay, let's get it over with," and joins him in a whining, groaning chorus, delivered in her best five-year-old voice. Parents of kids who love to rhyme and riddle can attack the dirty room dilemma by asking: "What do you get when you cross a greasy spoon and a dirty laundry bag?" Answer: "Your room."

One smart mom of a teenage daughter is committed to watching MTV for at least 15 minutes a week so that she can engage her daughter with references to song lyrics and singers. At a critical moment, she surprises her by singing a stanza from Madonna or by bargaining: "You can listen to Milli Vanilli full-blast while you vacuum the living room."

Listen to a wonderful example of the power of the flip side of speaking your kid's language—that is, *sending your message in another language*. Marilyn H., 45, had come to terms with the fact that her 18-year-old daughter was sexually involved with her boyfriend. She was reassured by the fact that her daughter was responsible about birth control, but she was uncomfortable with the idea that the couple's love-making sometimes took place in her home.

Here is how she successfully set her limits by describing the situation in a Yiddish phrase. "Sharon," she asked her daughter, "do you know what *shtupping* means?" "Yes," answered her daughter. "Well, honey, I understand that you and Steve are very involved with each other, but I don't want you *shtupping* in my house!" "Alright, Mom," laughed Sharon.

FAMILY FUNNIES: A PRACTICE SESSION

Pause and remember the moments when your child's behavior made you want to run away from home. Practice a lighthearted response to bring a bit of comedy to the clash.

PRACTICE

Your five-year-old's bedtime has become a battlefield. You bid her goodnight and come back 30 minutes later to find her dancing on the ceiling. How might you use humor to put your night owl to sleep?

Hint: Try the art of overstatement. At bedtime, bring an armful of toys and books to her bed and announce, "Tonight I want you to stay up all night. I'll be back in an hour to make sure you are still up." P.S.: In order for this to work, you may have to survive several long nights.

What other approaches will work for you?

PRACTICE

Picture yourself fuming as your teenager is in the middle of a third marathon phone call and you need to use the phone. How can you clear the line–without pulling the plug from the wall?

Hint: Try the art of understatement to gain attention. You might say, "Honey, I found out I won the million-dollar lottery today and I'm expecting a call about where to pick up the money."

What other variations will work for you?

With your youngest children, you might try a more direct route to laughter. Elaine R., 29, and her husband refer to their willful 3-year-old daughter as "Alexis" (the Joan Collins vixen on the now-defunct TV soap "Dynasty"). "When she is cranky or stubborn, we just start to tickle her; and just like the research says, when she laughs, she stimulates the release of her endorphins—we can watch those happy hormones change her mood on the spot!"

OUT OF THE MOUTHS OF BABES: WHAT YOUR CHILDREN CAN TEACH YOU ABOUT LIGHTENING UP

Lily Tomlin's childish character, Edith Ann, was among her most popular comic creations. Sitting in an oversized rocking chair, Tomlin as Edith Ann offered her clear view of adult life with the punchline "and that's the truth," followed by a raspy Bronx cheer. Sometimes the quickest path to light parenting is allowing yourself to be drawn into the good humor of your children who, like Edith Ann, refuse to see the somber world of the adult and offer a fresh perspective on your problems.

Marcia C., 32, an attorney, explains, "My daughter has such a great belly laugh, she's the one who taught me to lighten up. When I see the world through her eyes, it just looks funnier."

You might follow the example of one father who taped TV's Mr. Rogers each day on his VCR. As part of a lightening-up ritual at the end of the workday, he would

• •

watch it with his son. "Just watching the goofy Mr. Rogers put on his cardigan for the millionth time and hearing him sing 'It's a beautiful day in the neighborhood' helps adjust my attitude," he says.

Allow yourself to be cheered and comforted by the good humor of your children of all ages. Listen as these kids help their parents lighten up.

> *A "theory of relativity" from a five-year-old listening to his parents who have both been laid off from their jobs:* "Sometimes, there are just no cartoons on TV."

> *The repartee of the 10-year-old being chased around the living room by her mom:* "You know, Mom, you didn't raise a dumb kid. Do you really think I'm going to stop and let you catch me?"

> *A sensitive 12-year-old attempting to comfort his mother, who had just had a mastectomy:* "But, Mom, you really don't need two; they are just for decoration."

> *A 20-year-old daughter interrupting her mother's nagging mid-sentence with a comic New Age comparison:* "Mom, have you been going to Shirley MacLaine's seminars? You sound like you're channeling Grandma!"

Allen Klein, humor educator and the editor of *The Whole Mirth Catalog*, tells the story of a woman whose son helped her gain perspective on her setbacks. She had recently separated from her husband, her company had been sold, and her car needed a new battery. Just when she thought she couldn't handle another thing, her water heater exploded. As she stood examining the damage, her son walked into the basement, saw the mess, and proclaimed: "Oh, good, we're having another adventure!"

Ask any mom. She will tell you that family life is the funniest business she knows.

*E*PILOGUE:

··

THE TRIUMPH OF
THE GOOD-HUMOR WOMAN

*E*verywhere I look, I see a potential good-humor woman. Last week, she was walking confidently in my direction, wearing an elegantly patterned suit and a smart silk shirt. In one hand she held a briefcase, in the other a chocolate ice cream cone that she was enjoying with the relish of a young girl. What she didn't know was that a dribble of brown ice cream had settled on her lovely shirt. As she passed me, I had the fantasy that when she discovered the stain–even if she was in the middle of an important meeting–she would simply smile to herself and carry on.

*R*ESULTS OF THE *M*ACKOFF *N*ATIONAL *S*URVEY OF *G*OOD-*H*UMORED *W*OMEN

It has been five years since I started researching this book, I've met many good-humored women and numerous others who are determined to stop hiding behind their oh-so-serious selves. Recently I decided to survey 300 business-women across the country to find out where they stand on the issue of lightening up.

The results were remarkably encouraging. In answer to the question: *Do you feel you have lightened up and have more of a sense of humor than you did three to five years ago?*, a whopping 87 percent said yes. Of those who had lightened up, 82 percent said they were able to laugh at their mistakes; 76 percent said they had begun using humor to defuse stressful situations on the job; 75 percent said lightening up included taking themselves less seriously; and 64 percent said they had stopped trying to be perfect.

Listen to how these good-humor women talked about lightening up in philosophical as well as practical terms:

> *Margaret G., 33, a consultant:* "It takes so much *less* energy to be lighthearted and have a sense of humor than it does to be 'too serious' or angry."

> *Ruth S., 44, a contractor:* "My work life has become much more relative. I ask myself: 'Will it matter a month from now?' "

> *Elisa M., 55, a sales manager:* "I try to find the funny side of a bad situation on the job. Life is too short to wear it like a stuffed shirt."

I hope that as you have read, you have accepted the challenge of lightening up and nurturing your unique sense of humor. I hope, too, that you will abandon the beliefs about successful women that prevent you from reaching your potential—and embrace some powerful new alternatives.

The Successful Woman: Five Powerful New Beliefs

FORMER BELIEF #1:
SHE CAN'T BE FUNNY
(OR SHE WON'T BE TAKEN SERIOUSLY)

As a successful professional woman, you must make a serious commitment to humor. Like Phyllis R., 44, an entrepreneur, you can use humor as a communication tool. "I run my own business," explains Phyllis, "and when my attitude is lighter, the contact with clients is more effective." Like Nancy K., 35, a sales director, you know that laughter is the best management. Says Nancy, "With my lighthanded approach, I have been able to successfully unite six diverse personalities into a cohesive work team."

NEW BELIEF: A SUCCESSFUL WOMAN USES HUMOR AS A POWERFUL PROFESSIONAL TOOL.

FORMER BELIEF #2:
SHE STRIVES TO BE PERFECT
(SHE CAN'T AFFORD TO BE WRONG)

As a savvy businesswoman, you are learning to avoid the pitfalls of perfectionism and to remain composed amidst the comedy of your errors. Your attitude may be like Jackie A., 31, an engineer, who was relieved to find that "nothing really changes if everything I do isn't perfect." Or like Eva S., 46, an attorney who now enjoys "seeing the humor in my errors; my image doesn't have to be crystal-clear to succeed. We all make mistakes."

NEW BELIEF: A SUCCESSFUL WOMAN CULTIVATES LIGHTNESS AS AN ATTITUDE; SHE SHOWS GRACE UNDER PRESSURE.

••

FORMER BELIEF #3:
SHE MUST HIDE HER FEMININE SIDE

As a woman on her way to the top, you've taken a lesson from Mona Lisa and learned to convey a comfort and acceptance of yourself as a woman–often in the form of good humor. Your experiences may echo those of Lorraine K., 39, an accountant, who explains, "I've learned to accept myself as I am; my humor is an expression of my authenticity." You may identify with Helen N., 32, a real estate agent, who says, "Humorous women have an ease that other women don't. When I allow myself to be light, I connect with people on a different wavelength."

NEW BELIEF: A SUCCESSFUL WOMAN PRACTICES THE ART OF BEING AT EASE WITH HER POWERFUL PRESENCE AS A WOMAN.

FORMER BELIEF #4:
SHE AWAYS ATTACKS SEXISM
(SHE MUST BE ON GUARD)

As a smart and funny woman, you have discovered how mirth can work to manage sexual tension, and you know the difference between sexual heckling and sexual harassment. You probably agree with the decision of Roberta T., 47, a government administrator: "I like to distinguish between men who are hopeless and ones who can be rehabilitated." You'll also enjoy the observation of psychologist Carol Tavris: "For the small indignities of life, the best remedy is a Charlie Chaplin movie; for the larger indignities, fight back. And learn to tell the difference."

NEW BELIEF: A SUCCESSFUL WOMAN CHOOSES HER BATTLES WITH MEN WISELY.

To these four new beliefs, we must add another. In the process of lightening up, you have expanded your definition of success and discovered the importance of taking the balance and perspective of your good humor beyond the boundaries of your office.

On-the-job humor is an indispensable professional tool; at home, humor is the quickest road to self-renewal, one that deepens our connections with the people we love. You can understand what Tracy K., 32, means when she says, "On the days when life at work is especially tense, I can't wait to come home and unwind by laughing about it with a close friend." You may also recognize what Amy T., 43, is feeling when she predicts, "I expect to survive my daughter's teenage years solely on the strength of my sense of humor."

NEW BELIEF: A SUCCESSFUL WOMAN CHERISHES HER SENSE OF HUMOR IN BOTH HER PROFESSIONAL AND PERSONAL LIFE.

What a pleasure for me, in writing this book, to meet so many good-humored women and to have the opportunity to persuade you to become one. As I wrote, each chapter served as a reminder to continue to value the lightness in my own life. (Don't think for a moment that I don't need friends and family to tell me, "It looks like you need to lighten up about this.")

The powerful women who have spoken from these pages are testimony to the urgency of adding a sense of humor to your professional portfolio. The triumphant, good-humored women I have met have convinced me that we can continue to lighten up—without changing our politics or our professional purpose.

Won't you join us?